Monte Foreman's
Horse-Training Science

MONTE FOREMAN'S HORSE-TRAINING SCIENCE

by

MONTE FOREMAN

and

PATRICK WYSE

UNIVERSITY OF OKLAHOMA PRESS

NORMAN

BY MONTE FOREMAN

Horse-handling Science (Fort Worth, 1948)
Cantankerous Leads (Birmingham, 1966)
(with Patrick Wyse) *Monte Foreman's Horse-Training Science* (Norman, 1983)

BY PATRICK WYSE

Horse Psyching for Problem Horses (Conrad, Montana, 1983)

Library of Congress Cataloging in Publication Data

Foreman, Monte, 1915–
    Monte Foreman's Horse-training science.

    Includes index.
    1. Horses—Training. I. Wyse, Patrick, 1935–   II. Title.
SF287.F66   1983   636.1'3   82–40450

The paper in this book meets the guidelines for permanence and durability of the Committee on Production Guidelines for Book Longevity of the Council on Library Resources, Inc.

To the memory of

Charley Russell
Will Rogers
and
Will James

They were good for me.

MF

Contents

Foreword

After you have one leg on the left side, your other leg on the right side, and your mind in the middle, the next thing is to learn how to ride and guide. Until now books on riding technology have been scarce, but in the beginning-to-end sequence photographs in this book you will see how it is done.

Beginning in 1943, my motion-picture research has documented the science of move-basics—the technology of efficient horse-and-rider performance. This performance science is not exclusively for western, gymkhana, and other speed events but is equally effective when applied to its ultimate usefulness—in jumping, dressage, and polo. What is more, it saves months of training time.

By 1945, I had professionally ridden more than 25,000 horses on cow ranches, on race-tracks, in rodeos, with the United States Cavalry, and on jump courses and polo fields. Gradually I became aware that riding technology was more or less harmonious in working essentials.

When I was a lieutenant in the army and assistant director of the Visual Aids Department of the Horse Cavalry School, Fort Riley, Kansas, I learned how effective motion pictures could be in research and training. Complicated movements that were too fast for the

eye to analyze could be replayed in slow motion and studied. These were facts on film, not opinions.

Until that time only three lead move-basics had been documented. They were limited to the moves of slow, collected cantering. There was a great void in the science of getting, changing, and using leads at faster speeds; of 180-degree rolls; of off-the-seat, leanaway riding; or of calf-roping stops on ridden horses, as well as the importance of bits and saddle rideability. There was little understanding of the horse's reaction time or of how the rider's actions caused positive or adverse reactions by the horse. My film research added much to leads basics, revealing horse and rider agility needs and many more move-basics.

This information has been made available in booklets, training films, and videotapes. My accredited instructors and I have held more than 1,500 "Rider Science Clinics" throughout the United States and Canada, specializing in teaching riders on their own horses. As of this writing more than 75,000 students, each in less than twelve hours of instruction, have gained the ability to get and change leads at all speeds, perform 180-degree rolls, and make at least fair stops, with the confidence that with practice they can go on to make good ones.

More than thirty world champions in rodeo and horse-show competitions credit Foreman training for their achievements in reining, team roping, western riding, working cow horse, western pleasure, trail, gymkhana, polo, and jumping. Many of these champions appear in Foreman films and videotapes, and some of them are pictured in this book.

Many writers on horsemanship are long on words but short on experience and know-how. I am the opposite—long on "show-how" but short on words. If it were not for Pat Wyse's persistence and help with the writing, this book would probably not be in your hands today. My thanks to a helluva horse hand and instructor.

Five other persons helped very much: Doreen Wyse, Susette Curtis, Susan Baker, Johanna Fallis, and Beverlee Fields. My thanks to them all.

Monte Foreman

Elbert, Colorado

Preface

Monte Foreman's name will be recorded in the annals of history alongside the other great teachers of horse-training methods. His inquiring and tenacious mind, sometimes bordering on the prophetic, did not always please his peers. Twenty years ago many of his concepts were considered so radical that some authoritarian figures discounted them as improbable or impossible. Today those methods have been absorbed into multitudes of training approaches, bringing satisfaction and monetary reward to innumerable riders.

Monte Foreman traveled to the people and taught clinics in communities where no other horse-instruction opportunities existed, bringing with him the best and most current information available. These techniques were so thoroughly conceptualized that today, twenty to thirty years later, second generations of riders are successfully using Foreman methods learned from their parents. Beyond a doubt no other living person has had such an impact on horse and rider training and riding equipment.

Rarely does a man dedicate a lifetime to inquiring into a specific facet of human behavior as Monte Foreman has done. Although he is most often thought of as an expert with horses, his most enduring contribution has been to that special relationship that mankind has had with the horse for thousands of years. It has been this interaction of horse and rider that motivated Monte to devise the system of training documented in this book.

My role in the writing of this book began when I was a student of Monte Foreman's and continued when I became the first instructor to teach under his banner. After twenty years of training experience, including ten years teaching both in traveling clinics and in my school for breaking and training horses, I became a partner in this project.

The process of documenting move-basics in words and photographs has brought me full circle. That is, I returned to view Monte Foreman's work as a student. That experience has demonstrated to me that, no matter how successful the progressive teacher becomes, he must always retain the curiosity and open-mindedness of a student.

This book does not conclude the research that produced it but becomes a stepping stone for better understanding now and in the future.

Patrick Wyse

Conrad, Montana

Monte Foreman's
Horse-Training Science

1

The Foreman Philosophy of Training

Throughout this book the reader will be exposed to a science of training horses that has been documented and thoroughly tested by thousands of horse-and-rider teams. This technique is not the only way to train a horse. There are many disciplines of horsemanship and many excellent trainers. The Foreman method has used many of the functional techniques of other disciplines to construct a total system. Unlike other methods of teaching horse handling, this system has been scientifically tested. Over 75,000 students have been the proving grounds.

The major factor that has made this system scientific is the use of photoanalysis. Through this technique specific *move-basics* have been identified. These move-basics have been organized in the same progressive manner as that used in other sports instruction. For instance, in the teaching of skiing, the snowplow leads to the parallel turn; in the teaching of tennis, the backhand is an integral part of the game; and in the teaching of riding, the rollaway is part of the reining pattern and is also the cutting horse's primary move.

The horse and rider can learn each move-basic in progression until a level of skill is attained for a specific application. When this approach is used, both horse and rider work under less stress and strain. The team method allows more versatility—and much more fun.

Efficiency is the central theme of all move-basics. In today's world of competition the horses are so closely matched that the race will usually go to the most efficient. The off-balance horse will often end up being a little too slow.

It is best for the beginning rider to use a gentle horse so as to be able to concentrate on learning these new techniques. The basic steps in starting the green colt will not be discussed here; that is a subject for a separate book. Most riders are not experienced enough to start an unschooled horse until they have learned to ride well and demonstrate a basic handle on a trained horse.

Putting the "finish" on a horse requires far more skill and time than the gentling process. Every rider is a horse trainer; in fact, whenever a person rides a horse, he affects the animal's behavior—sometimes well, sometimes poorly. This will become apparent as we investigate the learning process of the horse. Every rider must learn how to motivate and control a horse for maximum efficiency. If the rider is only a passenger, the horse will often revert to his native ways, which may include getting rid of his passenger. Through good instruction anyone is capable of becoming a good hand with a horse. The better you ride, the more exciting, challenging, and fun the world of horses becomes. 🐎

2

The Physical Ability of the Horse

The first basic fact the rider must consider is that his horse is limited by his physical design. Some moves are easy and natural, while others are difficult and may cause the horse to become unbalanced. When a horse becomes unbalanced, his efficiency drops. The more difficult the move is for the horse, the more difficult it is to teach. This often leads to the wrong application of excessive force and creates unnecessary tension in the horse that can destroy the learning process. When the rider accepts the horse's limitations, riding and training techniques can be modified. The rider must adjust his ways to fit the horse's needs. The horse cannot change the rules of nature that insist that he move in a balanced manner.

Knowledge of the art of blending the rider's efforts and weight with those of the horse reveals how a rider should sit the horse. The horse can carry weight efficiently only in a very specific manner. Observe how the horse's own weight is distributed. The forequarters of a horse make up the heaviest section. The strongest part of the horse's back is that portion supported by the ribs and the breastbone. The weakest portion of the horse's back is the loin area, the small of the back. This area of the spine is supported only by long, weak muscles. The horse can best support the rider's weight when the weight is kept forward, over

the forequarters. It is a well-accepted fact that racehorses run faster and jumping horses jump higher when the rider is on the *rider's groove,* that area of the horse directly behind the forequarters. At this point the ribs taper to their narrowest width.

Watch a proficient rider gallop a horse bareback. He sits in the rider's groove because it is the most secure area. That is also true when one rides in a saddle. Being able to keep the legs in close contact with the narrowest part of the horse's barrel gives the rider the most security. Even a contesting saddle bronc rider stays on or in front of the rider's groove. Unfortunately, traditional stock saddles prevent this kind of security. In chapter 5, "Saddles," this problem is further explored.

Knowledge of the horse's ability to carry weight is mandatory. Sitting back in the saddle slows the horse, while moving weight forward increases the horse's speed. A horse usually does what is easiest for him.

Rather than discussing the amazing ability of the horse to move and turn, it is better to understand his limitations. When the rider understands these limitations, the effort and time necessary to modify riding and training technology becomes worthwhile.

When moving in a straight line, the horse usually carries his head in line with the direc-

Fig. 2.1. Observe from the horse's basic structure where it is easiest for him to carry the rider's weight.

tion of his body. When the horse is turned, he should move his head in the direction of travel so that his head and neck can function as his balancer. The horse is so vulnerable to an abnormal head position that he can be thrown to the ground by having his head twisted severely to one side. In every move he makes, especially at the gallop, his head position influences his efficiency. When he is turning, he must lead with his head to function at his best. When he lowers his hindquarters, as in a stop, he must raise his head and neck. If his head rises too high, he rears in the air. If his head is too low, he usually props on his front end.

Another major factor to consider is that a galloping horse moves his head in rhythm with his body. To achieve maximum efficiency, a rider must work his hands with this motion when executing any galloping maneuver, such as a stop, a rollaway, or a lead change. Because the rider needs gentle working contact with the horse's mouth for effective control, he must make these guiding efforts in rhythm. This is one principle of "good hands." When this natural head motion is restricted, it often causes tension in the horse.

In basic handling, the horse must use his balancer to advantage, so the rider must understand natural head position. Such head positions are seen in the agile moves of cutting horses and the efficient stops of calf-roping horses. As each move-basic is explained, the natural head position will be observed. 🐎

3

The Mental Ability of the Horse

We do not attempt to deal here with what is only vaguely understood about the intelligence of the horse. Rather, we emphasize the factors that we have identified through years of experience and study. It must always be remembered that the horse has basic instincts and reflexes for survival that cause problems in training. When we understand these, it is easier to anticipate a horse's reaction.

BASIC INSTINCTS

The Herd Instinct

The horse, by nature, prefers company. In the herd he is always safe, does very little work, gets help fighting flies, and even finds romance. Why should he want to leave the herd? To this day he usually doesn't. The rider must remember that other horses will always draw his horse like a magnet. It takes more pressure when he comes by the herd, barn, or gate, and this pressure must always be used well ahead of the moment the horse tries for the herd. Once a habitual herdbound horse has started his break back, it takes much more pressure to correct him. Stay ahead of the horse and enforce guidance before he commits himself.

The Instinct to Flee

This instinct is easily observed. All horses want to run from strange and seemingly threatening objects. Horses will usually not fight if they can escape. Survival has always demanded flight, and even the domestic horse of today retains this instinct. When a horse is confronted with a new object, he often regards it as threatening and tries to run away. The instinct to flee can cause problems with any horse. If the rider regards shying and bolting in this light, then the solution becomes less emotional. Rather than punishing the horse, it makes more sense to familiarize him with the object he fears. Most horses lose their fear when they discover that no harm will come to them.

The Instinct to Fight

When a horse cannot escape easily, his fighting instinct may emerge. A wild horse in a small corral with no avenue of escape will kick or bite at any object threatening his well-being. Even a gentle horse may react violently when he is suddenly confronted with what seems to be a threatening object. A fight can also be a major hazard if a person steps in the middle of a social discussion between two horses. For example, a rider may come too close behind another horse and rider and get kicked. The kick was intended for the horse, not the rider, but that will be little consolation on the trip to the hospital.

The Instinct to Resist Pressure

This instinct is both the most important and the least understood instinct that riders must deal with daily. All animals react to a pull or push by resisting. Through training they can be taught to yield to this pressure. The most obvious example can be seen when a halter is placed on a colt for the first time. The colt pulls back when the trainer pulls ahead and moves forward only after he discovers how to escape from the discomfort of the halter. That is the key in teaching a horse to yield to pressure. Allow him, by showing him, a way to escape from the pressure. Reward him by releasing the pressure. To pull and release is the key, *not* just to pull. The horse always resists pressure with his legs, his head, and his entire body until he is conditioned by training to do otherwise.

In every occasion of guiding a horse, apply pressure to direct the horse and release pressure to reward the horse for going the desired direction. Remember, the harder you pull, the harder the resistance will be. Always start easy and apply no more pressure than needed to accomplish the desired result. The resistance to pressure always exists to some degree, and training must be continuously geared toward teaching the horse to "give."

Horses have many other instincts for survival, but these are the major ones that the rider-trainer must always take into account.

The horse's lack of ability to reason is the primary learning limitation that the rider must always remember. Too often a rider attempts to educate a horse at the same level that he would educate another human being. When an animal is credited with human intelligence, then all sorts of problems arise. The animal must be corrected at the moment of disobedience if the correction is to be effective. Lack-

ing the ability to reason, the horse learns almost totally through experience. If something hurts, he won't do it. If doing it satisfies his native drives, he attempts to do it again. When a rider accepts the premise that a horse does not reason, then training can become systematic and scientific. Understanding the basic instincts and limitations of the horse will take the anger and impatience out of training sessions.

THE CONDITIONED REFLEXES

Positive Conditioning

Horses, as well as human beings, learn through the process of conditioned reflex. This fact was first documented by the Russian scientist Ivan Pavlov. He placed several dogs in individual cages and hung a bell over each cage. Before feeding each dog, he would first ring the bell. At the sight of the food the dog would salivate in anticipation of eating. The amount of saliva was carefully calculated, and all the controls of a scientific experiment were used. Soon it was observed that the ring of the bell caused the same salivation as the sight of the food. No food was necessary to produce salivation —just the sound of the bell. The dog was conditioned by continuous and constant positive repetition until the reflex developed.

Another example of a positive reward for responding to a signal is catching a horse in a pasture with grain. This is also an application of Pavlov's experiment. The sound of grain rattling in the bucket is the signal. The horse coming to you is the desired reaction, and the grain is the reward. This response must be learned by the horse. A wild horse, hearing the rattle of grain, would probably spook and run away. Positive rewards must be used so that desired results can be easily achieved. Obviously, guiding a horse with a carrot dangling from a stick is not accepted in the show ring, so another method of conditioning a horse to respond must be used.

Avoidance Conditioning

This is the conditioning by which performance horses that possess a great amount of polish are trained. The shuttle-box experiment with dogs documents this reaction. Scientists built a box containing two compartments with a center wall low enough for a dog to jump. A mild shocking device covered the floor of each compartment, and a signal light was placed on each wall. A dog was placed in one side of the box. The light in that compartment was turned on, a few seconds went by, and then the shocking device was activated. The dog soon associated the signal light with the mild shock and learned to jump to the other side of the box before being shocked. In this way the dog was conditioned to avoid the unpleasant shock. It was also observed that without either the warning light signal or the necessary reaction period the dog became neurotic. Throughout this experiment the dog remained calm as long as consistent technique was utilized.

Another way of controlling an animal is through physical force. For example, with horses we accomplish this by pulling on the head and causing the horse to turn. Force may be necessary in the very initial stages of training. As the trainer develops skill, however, force should be minimized and the conditioned reflexes strengthened.

The principles of conditioned reflex can be applied to the training of horses. The horse learns to avoid the hard pulls on the bit or the discomfort of a bat and spur by reacting to a cue (signal), not physical force. As the desired reaction is achieved, the strength of the cue is diminished until the horse appears to perform as an extension of the rider's mind.

Reaction Time

This natural phenomenon is always present and must always be considered. All animals have reaction time. An example of reaction time in human beings can be observed when the driver of a car sees a ball suddenly roll into the street. The time it takes for his central nervous system to signal his foot to move from the gas pedal to the brake pedal is the reaction time. This phenomenon must be considered in horse handling. When a horse is signaled to react, the rider must allow time for the horse to interpret the signal and move his muscles accordingly. It is essential to allow for reaction time if the conditioned-reflex system is to be used. Without consideration of reaction time the horse is controlled through force alone. He has no opportunity to learn. As in all trained athletes reaction time diminishes with consistent training, but it never disappears. The cue (signal) plus reaction time plus needed enforcement equal efficient horse handling. Consistency is the key to a polished performance. If the sequence is altered through a cue change, the reaction time will diminish. To produce a well-trained horse, the rider must always be alert in his handling. Nothing can be done casually. Every move must be planned well ahead. Reaction time must be allowed for, and no more force than needed should be applied. The last is critical because it prevents a horse from souring.

Reinforcement

Another important factor in conditioned reflex is *reinforcement*. It is merely "tuning the horse up" when his reactions become less keen. The rider goes back to the earlier training techniques of a strong cue and a more vigorous use of enforcement until the horse reacts as desired.

Memory in the horse, as in man, is the ability to retain past experiences. It is the best indicator of the horse's capacity to learn. All other factors being constant, the horse should remember what occurred yesterday and react in a similar manner today. The horse that reacts with less pressure today than what was needed yesterday has the ability to remember. The more intelligent and sensitive the horse, the quicker he learns both good and bad habits. The smarter the horse, the better the trainer has to be.

The horse's sensitivity is a factor all riders must consider. Some horses are very sensitive to pain. Such horses will react to hurt in a negative way. What would be an ordinary pull on the bit or use of a spur on most horses might cause a severe reaction in the highly sensitive horse. Many of these unusually sensitive equines have the ability to be tremendous performance horses. Too often they are spoiled beyond any hope of salvage because their extra sensitivity was not recognized in the beginning. Feel your horse and be a student of his reactions, using no more force than necessary for that particular animal.

Remember that you must be consistent with cues, give adequate reaction time, and use enforcement. This method of training a horse opens a new world of excitement and efficiency in horse handling. 🐎

4

Bits and Bit Accessories

The selection of equipment for training your horse is extremely important. An inferior bit prevents the use of the best training techniques, just as a saddle that fails to provide the rider the security that is needed makes it harder to control the horse with any precision.

The Foreman equipment was developed over many years to correct the deficiencies in horse-handling gear seen in clinics with 75,000 horse-and-rider teams. It became a question of getting the right bits, accessories, and saddles for these riders or watching them strangle and fail in a mire of nonfunctional equipment. Some of this equipment was not only inadequate but dangerous to both horse and rider. The criteria for good riding equipment are that it must be humane, versatile, and efficient.

🐎 BITS

Two main types of bits are used to control horses (a few special-use bits will be discussed separately). These two types are classified by function.

Nonleverage (Snaffle) Bit

The nonleverage bit has no shank or leverage attachments. The design of the mouthpiece does not determine the type of bit: nonleverage bits can have a variety of mouthpieces—jointed, solid, bar, port, wrapped, and so on. The *U.S. Horse Cavalry Manual* calls nonleverage bits *snaffles,* as do hunter-jumper and

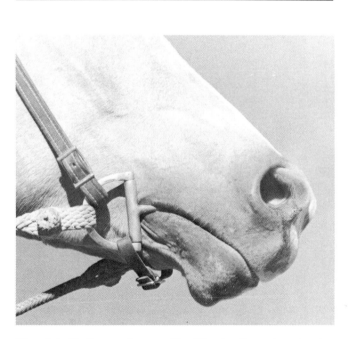

Fig. 4.1. *D-ring racing snaffle.* The leather strap under the horse's chin prevents the sides of the bit from being pulled into the mouth when lateral force is used.

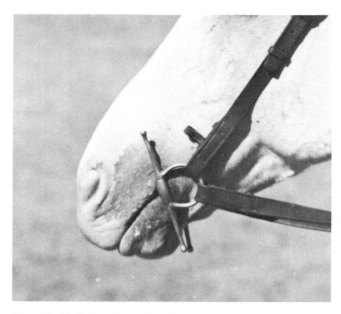

Fig. 4.2. *Full-cheek snaffle.* The long sidepieces prevent pulling this bit into the horse's mouth. No chin strap is necessary. Our experience has shown this bit to be the most effective of the non-leverage bits.

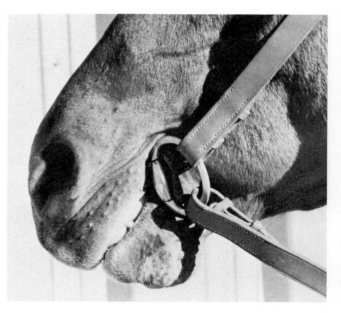

Fig. 4.3. *Egg-butt ring snaffle.* Another commonly used bit that is fairly efficient.

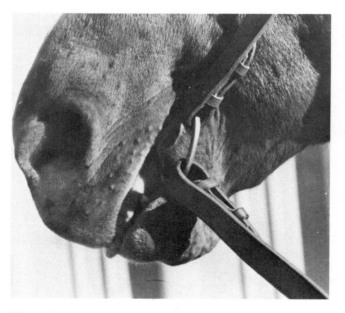

Fig. 4.4. Ring snaffles and even D snaffles can be pulled into the horse's mouth when no chin strap is used. The smaller the ring, the easier the bit will pull into the horse's mouth when use of force is necessary.

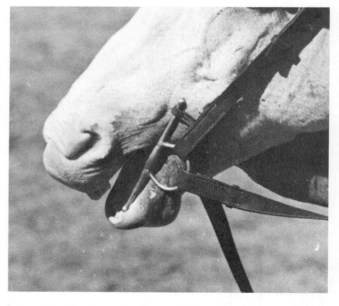

Fig. 4.5. The full-cheek snaffle's effectiveness is destroyed when the upper sidepiece of the bit is hobbled to the headstall, as often seen in show-ring classes.

polo riders. No bit with leverage shanks should be called a snaffle. Examples of good nonleverage bits are D-ring (or dee-ring) and full-cheek snaffles, as shown in *figures 4.1 and 4.2.*

Nonleverage (snaffle) bits give the rider maximum *lateral control*—the ability to turn the horse's head toward the direction you want him to go. With a bit such as a D-ring or full-cheek snaffle the rider can force a horse, if necessary, to turn his head *(see chapter 6, "The Rider").* Only a nonleverage bit gives the rider maximum lateral control. The lack of lateral control can be observed in many photographs of leverage bits in action.

The nonleverage (snaffle) bit is the most effective bit to use on green colts. The rider is able to turn the colt's head to prevent him from running or bucking. It is also a basic tool for correcting head-position, flexion, and control problems in older horses. In our clinics we have used nonleverage bits thousands of times for correcting problems with older horses. We have had consistent results in quieting horses that have been hurt through the use of severe bits. It is amazing what a trained rider can accomplish with a snaffle bit even on a tense, excited horse.

Throughout the useful lifetime of the horse the rider will encounter periods that require reinforcement of basic handling. Without good lateral control the horse and rider are handicapped in all guiding efforts. The rider is safer on a horse that turns willingly, and the nonleverage bit is the best tool to accomplish this goal.

Leverage (Curb) Bit

A *leverage bit* has shanks that mechanically increase the strength of the force on the reins. It is necessary to use a curb strap or a flat curb chain with this bit for proper action.

The amount of leverage is determined by the length of the lower shank *(figure 4.6b)* as related to the length of the upper shank *(figure 4.6a).* If the lower shank is equal in length to the upper shank, the leverage is called "1 to 1." If the lower shank is twice as long as the upper

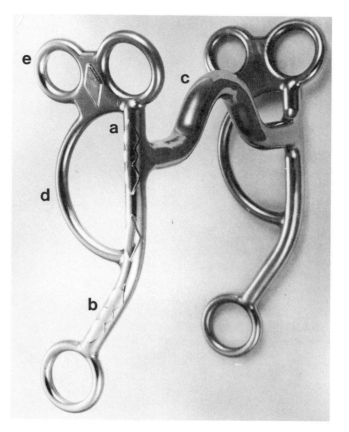

Fig. 4.6. The five parts of the Foreman Versatile Leverage Bit. The shank consists of *(a)* the upper shank, *(b)* the lower shank, *(c)* the mouthpiece (the dividing line), *(d)* the snaffle ring, and *(e)* the nonpinch curb loop.

shank, the leverage is referred to as "2 to 1." The longer the lower shank, the less effective lateral-control efforts will be, because the longer lower shank increases the contradictory pain when the rider tries to force the horse to turn.

The mouthpiece *(figure 4.6c)* comes in a variety of designs. The straight or slightly curved mouthpiece puts most of the pressure on the horse's tongue. A medium port (upward curve), as found in most Foreman bits, allows a portion of the tongue to go into the port. This distributes the pressure half on the tongue and half on the space in front of the molar teeth in the lower jaw (commonly known as

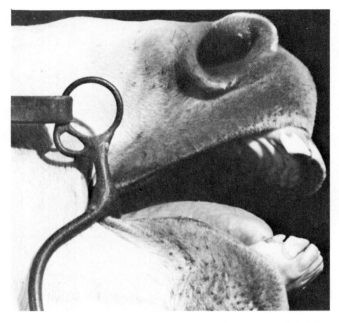

Fig. 4.7. Bits with a long upper shank cause painful lip stretching. Since the headstall will not stretch, the lip must, prying the mouth open excessively.

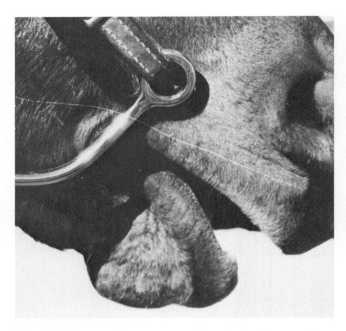

Fig. 4.8. Lip stretching causes a flare in the lip, resulting in wrinkles. The longer the upper shank, the more it stretches the mouth.

Fig. 4.9. When the curb strap or chain is too loose, the pinching becomes more apparent.

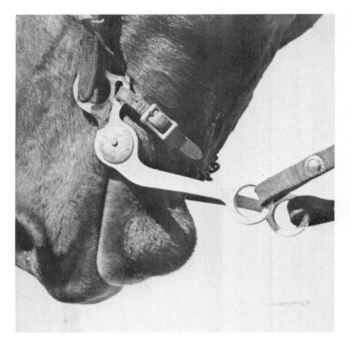

Fig. 4.10. Even with the separately set curb slot, this aluminum curb pinches the lip between the shank and the curb strap.

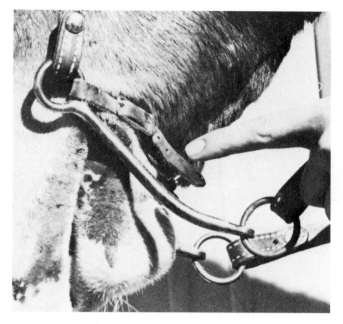

Fig. 4.11. This rounded steel curb pinches with the slightest amount of rein contact.

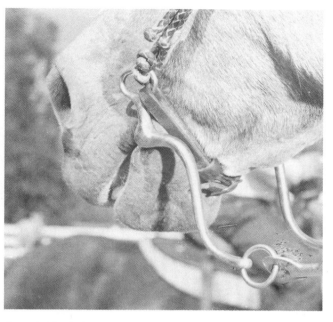

Fig. 4.12. This bit with the slightly shaped-out upper shank still pinches.

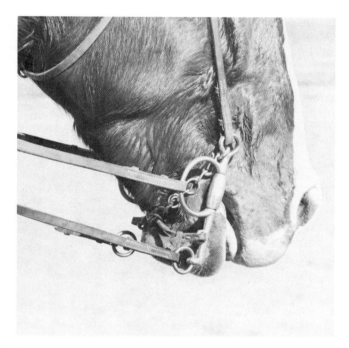

Fig. 4.13. This egg-butt Pelham is also an offender. Note the curb chain's pinching position against the lip.

the *bars*) of the horse's mouth. This particular port works well on a high percentage of horses. A higher and wider port forces more of the horse's tongue into the port to bring more force down on the bars, the most sensitive area.

Most leverage (curb) bits lacking drop-back nonpinch curb loops will painfully pinch the lip between mouthpiece and curb strap. To test your bit for pinching, simply pull the lower shank back up and above the saddle horn to simulate rein action and check to see if the bit has pinching possibilities. The bits shown in *figures 4.10 to 4.13* did not pass the test.

The Foreman Versatile Bit

So many and varied devices are used to control a horse that they could be the subject of an entire book. Most of the bits and hackamores illustrated here have been observed in action in Foreman clinics. Very few of them work well. Every bit should function in such a

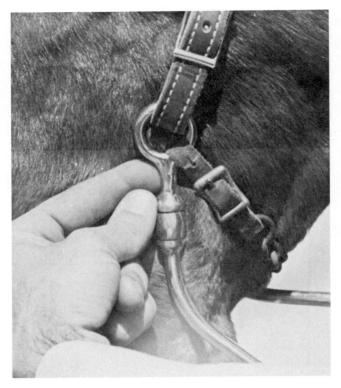

Fig. 4.14. This jointed mouthpiece, loose-jaw leverage (curb) bit, has been miscalled a "cowboy snaffle." The short upper shank causes extremely painful lip pinching.

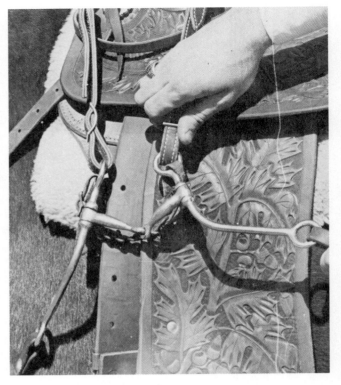

Fig. 4.15. The action of the jointed mouthpiece in combination with the loose-jaw swivel cheek creates more problems. A lateral pull on the lower shank causes the upper shank to gouge the horse's lip against the teeth.

manner that the horse could be physically forced to respond if force should become necessary. The manner in which the bit affects the horse must be humane and must not cause sharp, sudden pain, which destroys control and good training. The Foreman Versatile Bit *(figures 4.21 to 4.31)* was developed with the goal of humane control in mind.

Special-Use Bits

The bits shown in *figures 4.32 to 4.37* have limited and special applications. The designs function in a manner that restricts their use on most horses. They can, however, serve useful purposes in training horses.

🐎 ACCESSORIES TO IMPROVE BIT FUNCTION

Three basic accessories are used to improve the function of bits. The *running martingale (figure 4.38)* prevents the horse's mouth from being stretched. The mouthpiece pulls on the bars instead of the horse's lips. It is essential with a nonleverage (snaffle) bit, but it is also efficient in use with a *combination bit (see figure 4.26)*. The *drop noseband (figure 4.42)* helps prevent the horse from learning to open his mouth to escape the pressure of the bit. The *tie-down (figure 4.43)* is used with gag bridles and leverage hackamores to prevent the horse from evading the bit by raising his head excessively. 🐎

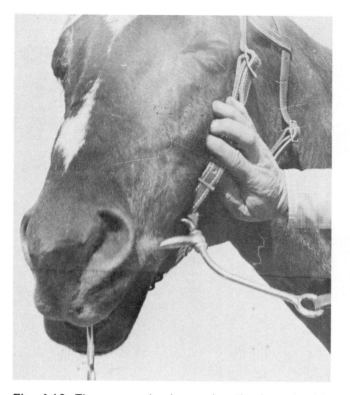

Fig. 4.16. The upper shank gouging the horse's skin against the teeth painfully contradicts the lateral control when used on the lower shank.

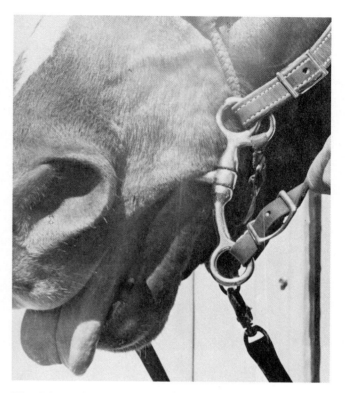

Fig. 4.17. This leverage (curb) bit has the same conflicting action as that shown in *figs. 4.14–4.16*, except that the lower shank is shorter. This bit is misnamed a "Tom Thumb snaffle." It is *not* a snaffle.

Fig. 4.18. When a rider attempts to use lateral control with force, all the bits in *figs. 4.14 and 4.15* cause the horse to throw his head in the air, fight for his head, and guide poorly.

Fig. 4.19. When the rider is trying to neck-rein with force, leverage (curb) bits invariably cause the horse to turn his head the wrong way. The resulting pressure always tells the horse to "whoa."

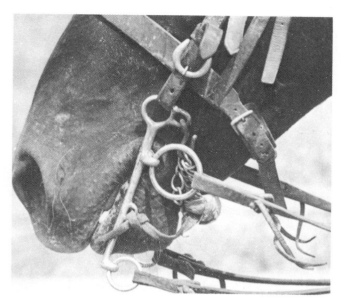

Fig. 4.21. The forerunner of the Foreman Versatile Bit. In the 1940s, Foreman had "nonpinch" curb loops welded onto his polo and training bits to relieve pressure on the lip area.

Fig. 4.20. Again, the flip of the head away from the direction you want to go and the pressure on the bit always makes the horse want to stop or fight his head, contradicting his natural agility.

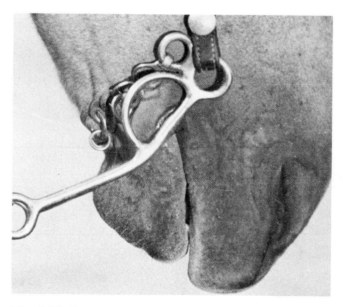

Fig. 4.22. Foreman nonpinch curb loops are set back far enough to allow adequate clearance of the lip wrinkles. Without lip stretching and pinching pain, horses give their heads and guide much more easily.

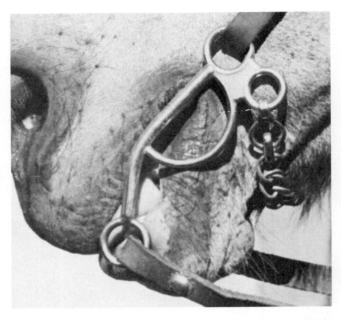

Fig. 4.24. The Foreman Versatile Bit offers many advantages for humane and efficient use. Here it is used as a leverage (curb) bit.

Fig. 4.23. Response to a light rein at speed requires an understanding of move-basics. Monte Foreman won second place on this horse at the National Appaloosa Championships. Shown here is Dennis Murphy, later a member of the 1978 United States Equestrian Jumping Team.

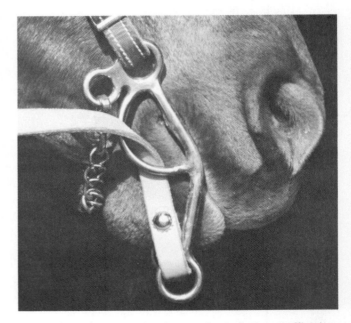

Fig. 4.25. Run the curb reins up through the snaffle ring or fasten the rein end to the snaffle ring, and you have a nonleverage (snaffle) bit, with the lateral control essentials.

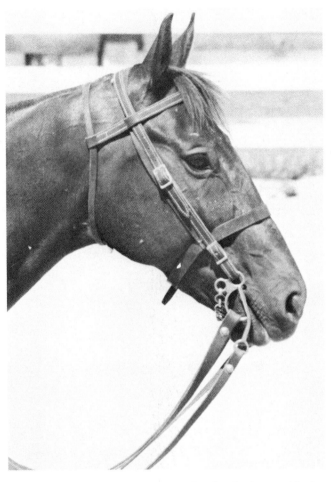

Fig. 4.26. In twenty-three years of polo playing and training, Foreman failed to see anyone play effectively on just a curb bit. The Foreman Versatile Leverage Bit, used as pictured here, gives leverage and lateral turnability.

Fig. 4.27. Monte Foreman training Chief of Four Mile, National Appaloosa High Point Performance Champion in 1955–56. The bitting used on this horse is shown in detail in *Fig. 4.21.*

BALANCED STOP

Fig. 4.28. This sequence *(with figs. 4.29 and 4.30)* shows a three-stride balanced stop taking place in approximately one second (note the position of the fence posts). Susan Baker riding Brush King, a Foreman demonstration horse.

Fig. 4.29. Only with superior equipment, training, and ability can such stops be accomplished by horse and rider. This series was taken during a Foreman Clinic demonstration in Indianapolis, Indiana.

Fig. 4.30. The balanced stop is the method that gives you great stops in a pile of rocks or the longest slide on good ground. This technique is thoroughly explained in chapter 13, "Balanced Stops."

Fig. 4.31. A no-hands stop by Susan Baker, instructor and demonstrator in the Foreman Clinics, on Brush King, riding a jump saddle and using a polo bridle, with a Foreman Versatile Bit. The stop is easy on horse and rider.

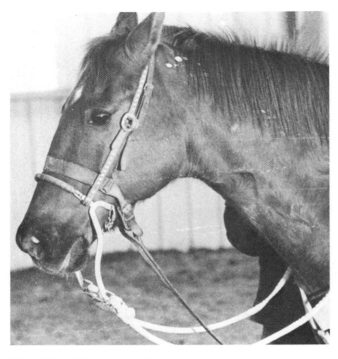

Fig. 4.32*a.* The mechanical leverage hackamore is generally limited to stopping a horse but works poorly for guiding with any force. It is often successful in use on calf-roping horses.

Fig. 4.32*b.* Jack Marr, Alberta, Canada, stops a difficult horse with a mechanical hackamore. The wide leather tie-down is adjusted to allow the horse's face to rise no more than parallel to the ground.

Fig. 4.33. *A gag bit.* The rope headstall slides through the top hole and bottom hole of the ring. It is effective in forcing the horse to raise his head and to retrain an insensitive or soured horse.

Fig. 4.34. When the reins are pulled, the bit slides up the rope, stretching the horse's mouth toward his ears. The strap (headstall) behind the ears has little or no effect.

Fig. 4.35. Combined with a leather noseband and tie-down, properly adjusted, the gag bridle is another effective tool to train a horse to stop.

Fig. 4.36. *Mouthpiece with a high port.* Any high port lets all of the horse's tongue go into the port so that when the bit is pulled the entire pressure is distributed on the bars of his lower jaw. Injury to the bars leaves scar tissue that has little feeling, resulting in a tough-mouthed horse.

Fig. 4.37. Some horses habitually get their tongues over the bit, making guiding much more difficult. Use of high port and roller helps correct this problem. The horse plays with the roller and acquires the habit of keeping his tongue under the bit. The high port makes it harder for the horse to get his tongue over the bit. The roller pictured here gives the same pressure as a lower port, half on the tongue and half on the bars.

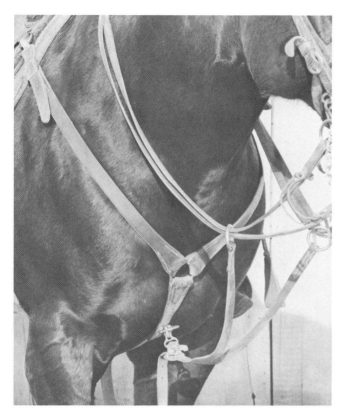

Fig. 4.40. Without a running martingale the bit pulls on the lips, causing the horse to throw his head in the air.

Fig. 4.38. *The running martingale.* This Foreman-designed running martingale hooks halfway between the breast-collar and the horse's underline, allowing for more and easier adjustment.

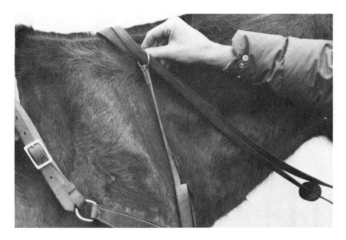

Fig. 4.39. The top of the running martingale ring should be parallel to the top of the shoulder blades. If adjusted higher, it will allow the horse to raise his head too high. If adjusted shorter, it makes the horse heavy on the fore-quarters.

Fig. 4.41. With a running martingale, adjusted as shown, the pull of the bit is on the bars of the horse's mouth instead of his lips. The bit works much more efficiently, and the horse guides better.

Fig. 4.42. *Drop noseband.* This accessory is used to keep the horse from opening his mouth. When introducing a horse to a drop noseband, do not put it on tight. After he gets used to it, tighten it reasonably.

Fig. 4.43. This type of tie-down works well with a gag bridle or leverage hackamore. The adjustment seen is a general rule of thumb. Wire or cable nosebands are too severe for most horses.

5
Saddles

The most important feature a saddle must have is rideability. Does the saddle put you in the best place to allow your horse to perform to the maximum of his ability? It can be the most beautiful saddle in the world, but it is useless if you can't ride it. Only by studying the relation of the rider to the horse, standing and in motion, from bareback through the different types of saddles, can we see what provides this rideability.

🐎 BAREBACK

When we study the shape of the horse's back it is easy to see where the rider fits naturally. This is the *rider's groove,* or *girth groove.* Only when we maintain position in the rider's groove are we able to stay securely with the horse. All true performance begins at this point.

🐎 TYPES OF SADDLES

Race Saddle

Riding for speed also makes use of the rider's groove. On both quarter horses and thoroughbreds jockeys ride with their stirrups hung in front of the cinch.

Race riders rode with long stirrups until the late 1880s, when the American jockey Tod Sloan began riding like a monkey on a stick. Everyone laughed at him, but he went to the

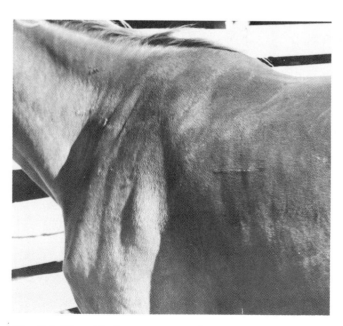

Fig. 5.1. The rider's groove, or girth groove, is the area where the horse's forequarters connect with the ribcage. This recessed channel allows the only security for bareback riders. This is where the rider must be.

Fig. 5.2. When the rider is in the right place, his legs fit into the rider's groove with enough leg-grip security to run, jump, and handle the horse. Monte Foreman shows where (HK Ranch, 1948).

Fig. 5.3. When the rider sits behind the rider's groove, he loses all leg and seat security, because of the roundness of the horse's barrel. Try it yourself. Foreman sits back.

pay window so often that all the other jockeys had to change to Sloan's style of riding to get back into the competition. Weight forward allowed the jockey to help the horse by carrying him over the horse's shoulders. The critical factor is to get where a horse can carry you easiest and fastest.

Jump Saddle

The stirrups are hung directly below the pommel on the jump saddle. The knee flaps *(see figure 5.9)* allow the rider to place his weight in front of his stirrups on the horse's shoulders.

Captain Federico Caprilli, of the Italian cavalry school, was the first to introduce forward riding into a system for all riders. Although the system became known as *forward seat,* the term is misleading. The system is really the balanced way of riding; the rider's seat is not a factor. The rider's seat does not touch the saddle from the start through the landing of

a jump. During the rising part of the jump the rider's weight is on the stirrups, and the security is from the knee through the bottom of the calf and stays constant through the landing. Leg security in the rider's groove allows harmony in motion from start to finish.

Riding the jump saddle in this manner, the rider is able to achieve the rideability needed to jump, ride cross-country, and perform so-called western stops.

Polo Saddle

On the polo saddle the stirrups are hung in the same place as on jockey and jump saddles. During play most of the rider's weight is carried on them. Because polo is a speed sport, the rider must be in a position for speed handling. His mount is called on for maximum effort over and over during periods of play. Polo ponies carry heavy men seven to eight minutes at a time with many wide-open races, quick stops,

Fig. 5.4. Security is necessary for handling. Gary Foreman spins AQHA Western Riding World Champion Teques Lady 81.

Fig. 5.5. Gary, age ten, on Wasta, age two, the tenth time Wasta was ridden. Note Gary's knees in the rider's groove, the only place to ride.

bumps, and turns. The secret is that the stirrups are far enough forward so that the polo player can brace in many directions yet stay in the center of the horse's balance. The stops and turns in western competition are much the same as those in polo.

Bareback Bronc Riding

In riding the bareback bronc the rider must sit forward of the girth groove to stay in balance with the wild twists, thrusts, and turns of the bucking horse. The bareback bronc photographs (figures 5.21 to 5.23) were taken at a rodeo in Colorado. Foreman was having trouble keeping his three-picture-a-second sequence camera in focus because the broncs were covering so much ground. He asked rider Casey Tibbs to spur his bronc on the left shoulder each stroke to try to make him buck in a circle so that the camera could stay in focus. This extraordinarily great bronc champion did it.

Bronc Riding Saddle

Again, the reason the stirrups are so far forward on a bronc saddle is to allow the rider to stay in balance with the horse. He can ride the horse when he hits the ground with his front feet. Most of the impact is absorbed in the rider's feet and legs. His stirrups, being in line with his body, keep him from being thrown off balance.

On the upward drive or jump of a bronc, forward-hung stirrups allow the rider's knees to stay in the same place, which is a must, for the knees are the only leg contact maintained throughout the ride.

Now that we have seen the security of the rider's groove and have proved with the camera where horses carry weight best and are ridden with the most rider security, let us compare these essentials with the rideability of traditional stock saddles.

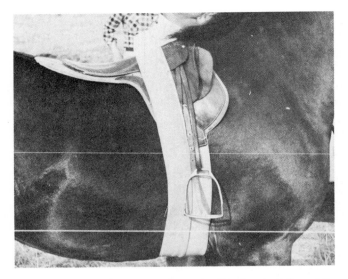

Fig. 5.6. Race stirrups are hung to the front of the girth groove, where weight is carried fastest and farthest.

Fig. 5.7. When the rider stands in the stirrups, all the weight is carried on the girth groove.

Ordinary Stock Saddle

There are two major problems with ordinary stock saddles. First, the stirrups are positioned too far back. Second, to compound the problem, the great bulk of the rigging also pushes the rider away from the rider's groove, defeating any attempt at security with the horse.

Since we must have rideability to achieve anything with our horses, it is important to study the saddle to see how it may hinder us from doing the job. Remember that the horse carries weight best in the rider's groove for maximum speed and performance. After studying this series of photographs, look at your sad-

dle. Is it giving you the rideability you must have?

Balanced Ride Saddle

As the Foreman research progressed, it became apparent that many of the moves we were seeking to make in the stock saddle could be made in the jump saddle or the polo saddle because such saddles put the rider in balance, in the rider's groove. The stock saddle had to have two main features to give it rideability. First, it had to have forward-hung stirrups to secure the rider in the rider's groove,

Fig. 5.8. When racing, jockeys crouch low to lessen the wind resistance, but the weight is still carried over the girth groove.

Fig. 5.9. Stirrups are hung at the front of the rider's groove. Janie Jones demonstrating.

where the rider could stand and move in constant balance with the horse. Second, it had to have bulkless rigging, to eliminate the problem of trying to maintain security on the horse through layers of leather, girth rings, and skirting between the rider's legs and the horse. To meet these requirements, the Balanced Ride "rigging" was created.

If your equipment is not giving you the rideability you need, improve your equipment, and you will improve your performance.

Over the past one hundred years horse trainer-writers have failed to present an accurate picture of how horses perform to their maximum ability. When compared to the high level of technology achieved in other sports—largely from study of motion pictures of the sport in progress—knowledge of horsemanship technology is far behind. The true horseman must always be wary of the blind acceptance of tradition, which has impeded progress in riding and guiding and the whole science of horse agility.

When we see what a difference an efficiently designed saddle makes in the performance of both horse and rider, it is obvious that the saddle plays an all-important part. All the design details of the Balanced Ride Saddle contribute to its rideability. They help the horse give his best possible performance.

Fig. 5.10. The knee through the lower calf maintains contact with the girth groove and provides leg-grip security. Susan Baker riding.

Fig. 5.11. The famous trainer Jimmy Williams's top hand, Sue Hutchinson, winning on Chestnut Hill at the California State Fair.

Fig. 5.12. Slippery Sam, a notoriously unguidable racehorse, responding to Susan Baker's knowledge and security in a jump saddle.

Fig. 5.13. The key to security is the knee through the calf in the rider's groove. Jeff Scheff on Tiny winning Senior Youth Activities Open Jumping at the AQHA Congress. (Jeff's mother, Sandra, is an accredited Monte Foreman instructor).

Fig. 5.14. During a Foreman Clinic in Indianapolis, Susan Baker performs a no-hands stop on Brush King, a Foreman demonstration horse.

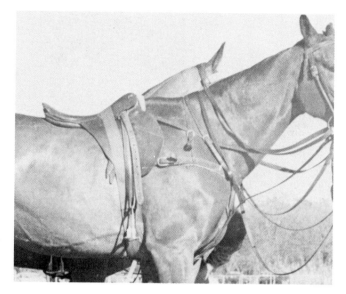

Fig. 5.15. Like race and jump saddles, the polo saddle has the stirrups hung at the front of the girth groove.

Fig. 5.16. When polo players stand, instead of being forced rearward, their feet and legs stay securely in the groove.

Fig. 5.17. Like roping, polo hitting is mostly done standing, off the seat, to get more power. Jackson, Wyoming, Polo Club.

Fig. 5.18. Monte Foreman played polo and trained polo ponies for twenty-three years in the bush leagues and the United States Cavalry and still insists that it is the greatest of the horse games. Jackson, Wyoming, Polo Club.

Fig. 5.20. In bareback bronc riding, the rider sits and hangs on above and ahead of the girth groove. Casey Tibbs, Professional Rodeo Cowboys Association World Champion Bronc Rider.

Fig. 5.19. Polo-type moves showing maximum handling agility during a clinic demonstration by Susan Baker on Brush King.

Fig. 5.22. Bronc-saddle stirrups are carried farther forward than all others, including race-saddle stirrups. The girth is against the horse's elbows, and the forward stirrup leather is secured ahead. This allows a free rearward spurring stroke without altering the rider's knee security.

Fig. 5.21. Horses can buck higher and harder carrying the weight here, but it is also the easiest place to ride.

Fig. 5.23. The forward position of the stirrups also enables the rider to meet the downward impact with his stroke, without moving his knees. Casey Tibbs, riding (he won eight bronc-riding titles and one all-around title).

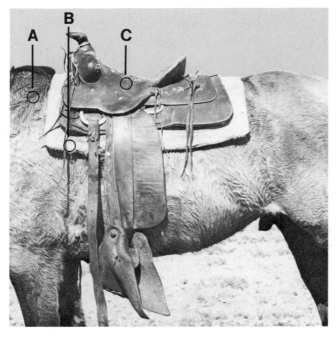

Fig. 5.24. The traditional stock saddle—instead of hanging the stirrups ahead of the girth like bronc saddles (position *A*) or race, jump, and polo saddles (position *B*) —has the stirrups back near the middle of the saddle seat (position *C*). The seat is also built up in front, which forces the rider to sit even farther back.

Fig. 5.25. Rigging bulk under the rider's legs hinders even more. Here is a thick rigging ring wrapped with six latigo thicknesses (three full wraps, which is average), creating more than 2 inches bulk under each knee. Imagine trying to ride with a 2-by-4-inch post under each knee.

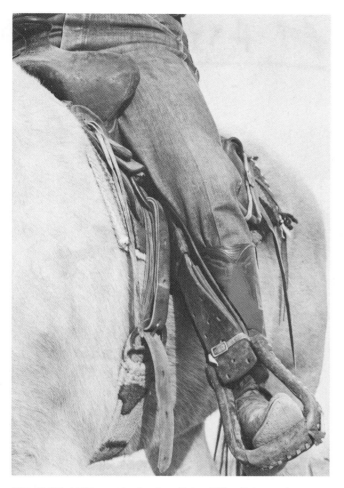

Fig. 5.27. It is impossible to stand and get the stirrup leathers over and in front of this bulk to use the girth groove leg grip as one can on race, jump, polo, and pro bronc saddles.

Fig. 5.26. With such rigging it is difficult to make contact with the horse's sides from the knee down. But even if the rider could do so, it would not give security because his legs would be on the horse's barrel, much too far back.

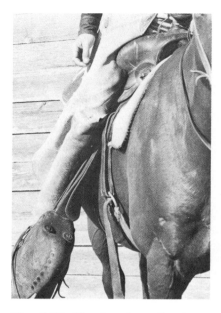

Fig. 5.28. The leg from the knee down cannot make contact with the horse's sides.

Fig. 5.29. The only contact with the horse's sides is from the knee up, which offers little grip or security. No rideability—just bouncing, flopping around, and hanging onto the saddle horn to keep a foot on each side and your mind in the middle.

Fig. 5.33. On a saddle like this, in order to stop, the rider must rear back, sit down, and yank on the reins. Alejandro Solis, HK Ranch, Texas.

Fig. 5.34. The rider's weight caves in the horse's back, making it extremely difficult for the horse to get his hind legs under his body. His so-called stop is stiff-legged, jarring, and awkward.

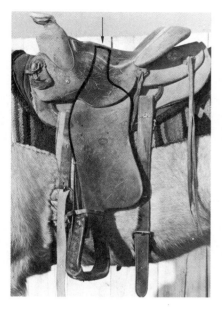

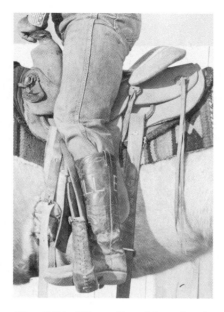

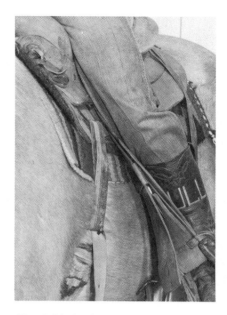

Fig. 5.30. Most stock saddles are built and ride basically the same way. Stirrups are hung a long way back of the rider's groove.

Fig. 5.31. When the rider stands in the average stock saddle, his weight is carried far behind the rider's groove, over the horse's barrel.

Fig. 5.32. In the average stock saddle the rider loses most of his security because he has no leg grip.

Fig. 5.35. Photoanalysis proved that Foreman was getting the same results. Horses consistently stopped stiff-legged, spread out, and on their front legs. Foreman on Chacho, Roswell, New Mexico. Chacho (Muchacho de Oro) was the sire of Nautical, famous United States Equitation Team jumper and star of the Walt Disney film *The Horse with the Flying Tail.*

Fig. 5.36. Foreman, experimenting for better results, tried sitting, which let him get his feet forward, then trying to meet stop impact.

Fig. 5.37. This procedure did not work well enough to produce good stops all the time, especially at high speeds. Foreman at the John Chisolm Ranch, Roswell, New Mexico.

Fig. 5.38. Fair stops were sometimes possible at a slow gallop, but never at high speeds. Foreman won first and second in senior AQHA reining at the New Mexico State Fair in 1948—first on Mister Hancock, and second on Del Monte. He also won the cutting contest, on Old Paint.

Fig. 5.39. As late as 1973 few trainers could do any better. Here is the winning ride in AQHA reining at Albuquerque, New Mexico, 1947.

Fig. 5.40. Photoanalysis showed that champion cutting-horse handlers had the same problems. Rearing back and sitting down on a cutting horse forces the horse down on his front legs, making him stiff-legged, rough, awkward, and inefficient. Foreman on Chacho.

Fig. 5.41. Foreman saddle experimentation begins to pay off. Here, riding Chacho straight up at Las Vegas, Foreman won second to world champion Buster Welch, on Chickasha Mike. (Walt Wiggins photo)

Fig. 5.42. In 1945 photoanalysis proved that everyone, including Foreman, was leaning way left, right, or backwards just to stay on and handle the horse.

Fig. 5.43. This "body English" not only looked terrible but caused a horse's performance to be awkward and out of rhythm and balance. Foreman on Butterfly.

Fig. 5.44. Leaning even this much makes many horses come out disunited or on wrong leads. Foreman on Chacho, left lead behind, but coming out on the right lead in front.

Fig. 5.45. When attempting same-lead rolls or rollaways at faster speeds, riders invariably lose their security or get left behind.

Fig. 5.46. Instead of getting down and coming out as a horse should, he "runs around the outhouse." Foreman training Mr. Hancock at the John Chisolm Ranch.

Fig. 5.47. In his search for better ways to stop in a saddle, Foreman went back to polo and jump saddles to stop on his stirrups instead of his seat and had much more success. Stops, rolls, and turns improved, giving the "handle-ability" he had experienced earlier in training polo ponies.

Fig. 5.48. This photograph and *fig. 5.47* were taken on the Richard King Cow Ranch, where Foreman (shown in *fig. 5.47*) and Alejandro Solis (shown above) broke and trained the remuda.

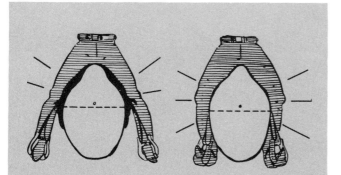

Fig. 5.49. *Left:* Diagram of legs on an ordinary stock saddle. Grip and fit are prevented below the knee, except with heels and spurs, which are not appreciated by the horse. *Right:* Legs on a Balanced Ride Saddle. Here is the grip and fit of jump, polo, and bronc saddles. Here is maximum security and rideability.

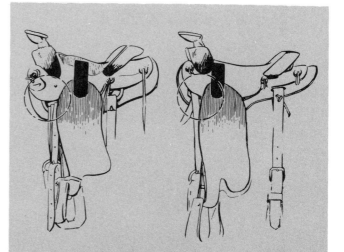

Fig. 5.50. *Stirrup positions. Left:* On an ordinary stock saddle. Although weight can be carried best in the vicinity of the circle, the stirrups on most stock saddles are hung far back on the seat. Even when standing, the rider does not get on the horse's "carrying circle." *Right:* On a Balanced Ride Saddle. Here stirrups are hung in the "carrying circle," where race, jump, polo and all other horses carry weight best.

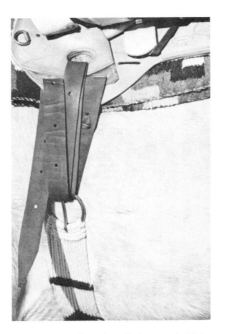

Fig. 5.51. Monte Foreman began experimenting to see what made jump, polo, and bronc saddles superior in balance, security, and rideability. Eleven years later, Balanced Ride Saddles were developed, patented, and trademarked. The countersunk bulkless riggings and forward-hung stirrups allowed grip and fit like this, even when the rider was standing.

Fig. 5.52. On the Balanced Ride Saddle the full double rigging is spread out and set higher, and is also very strong—we have never heard of such rigging, installed correctly, being jerked out.

Fig. 5.53. On the Balanced Ride Saddle the rider has leg-grip security in the girth groove all the way from his seat through his ankles.

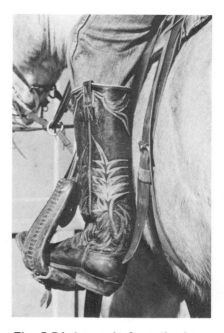

Fig. 5.54. Leg grip from the knee down through the bottom of the calf gives the most security, sitting or standing at all speeds, even during turns, rolls, stops, and other movements.

Fig. 5.55. On Balanced Ride Saddles stirrups are hung 4 to 6 inches farther forward than on "traditional" stock saddles, allowing the rider's legs to fit into the rider's groove.

BALANCED STOP

Figs. 5.56*A–C.* Photographs taken at three photos a second showing the terrific impact of a rough stop. ***A:*** The beginning of the stop.

Fig. 5.56 *B:* Young Gary Foreman's legs have no problem staying in the rider's groove and absorbing the jolt.

Fig. 5.56*C:* The stop ends with a fair stop in balance. Gary has no problem with rideability.

Fig. 5.57. Doug Milholland, a Foreman Clinic demonstrator and trainer, correcting a problem horse during a class. Note the security provided by the Balanced Ride Saddle.

Fig. 5.58. In the early 1950s, Foreman discovered that, by saying "Whoaa," releasing the reins, and then checking in stride when the horse's front feet were on the ground, he began getting consistent stops—stops in which the horses got down and slid behind with little pressure on the reins, while still running in front. This classic photograph of the world-famous Chappo Hancock was made during a Foreman Clinic in Rawlings, Wyoming, in 1954.

Fig. 5.59. On a "traditional" saddle the rider must try to thrust the feet forward over the bulky rigging and sit down to stay on. Note how the rider's weight caves in the horse's back, making it very difficult for him to get his hind legs up under his body.

Fig. 5.60. This is the result. In a very high percentage of rough, propped stops, caused by the rider's inability to stand in the rider's groove, the horse is unable to engage his hindquarters.

Fig. 5.61. The lack of rideability and security on a bulky "traditional" saddle is easily seen in photoanalysis. Here is an example of what the camera shows that the eye misses.

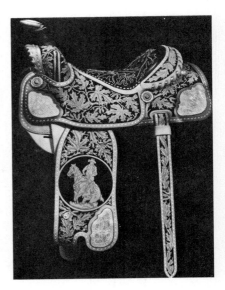

Fig. 5.62. All the Foreman-designed Balanced Ride Saddles have the same balance security and rideability. All stirrups are hung up front, and the bulkless riggings are very strong. *A:* Round fork.

Fig. 5.62*B:* A fork, or slick fork.

Fig. 5.62*C:* Swell fork.

Fig 5.63. The horse shown here is the polo stallion Woody D, owned by John Oxley, of the Tulsa Polo Club. Woody D was the star of the Disney film *Stormy.* The stirrups let out to fit six-foot-five Bill Hitt, shown here.

Fig. 5.64. The stirrups also adjust to fit Gary Foreman, ten years old. All Balanced Ride Saddles have a 14-inch adjustment.

Fig. 5.65. Foreman wanted his saddles to fit not only large and small people but large and small horses as well. This is a large, square-skirted trophy saddle on Wasta, a 50-inch Pony of America.

Fig. 5.66. Note how the latigos cinch up to fit Wasta.

Fig. 5.67. There is no problem cinching up on horses 16 or 17 hands. Susan Baker on Brush King, 16 hands and weighing over 1,300 pounds.

Fig. 5.68. Even in a propped stop, when the weight is carried in the rider's groove, the horse's back does not cave in. Foreman on Toots, Sawyer Cattle Company, Barnhart, Texas.

Fig. 5.69. Only when a horse's leading front leg is on the ground can the hindquarters come off the ground and arc to get farther under the body. The rider's weight in the groove makes this action easier for the horse.

Fig. 5.70. When the horse runs and the rider stands, it is great to have the security of the rider's groove.

Fig. 5.71. It is also great to be able to stand with security and pull on a horse's head without falling over frontwards or backwards.

Fig. 5.72. And it is great to feel your horse's hind end come up underneath you and begin sliding behind and running in front. Foreman training Toots.

Fig. 5.73. With rider security and effective rein handling, the horse is able to get down and hold behind. Foreman on Michael, owned by Lois Perry, of Greenwich, Connecticut. Michael was the fastest Arabian in the world and matched other Arabians at all distances winning all but 2 of 78 matches. He won the 100-mile Ocala Endurance Ride three times, retiring the trophy.

Fig. 5.74. On ordinary stock saddles, leaning the way you want the horse to go is necessary to stay on. Foreman training Euchucca Lad, Roswell, New Mexico.

Fig. 5.75. Leaning and wallowing around on the horse's back is detrimental to his handle-ability and agility.

Fig. 5.76. Photoanalysis and experience proved that if the rider's weight remains straight up or leans slightly away from the turn the horse is better able to get his hindquarters under him for more agility and balance. Foreman on a Balmy L colt.

Fig. 5.77. Riding balanced, the lean-away system applies to all turns. Most of the time the rider's seat is out of the saddle. This lean-away method cannot be accomplished without the leg-lock security of the rider's groove.

Fig. 5.78. Pacific Coast high-point gymkhana champion and Foreman accredited instructor John S. Huyler, of Ojai, California, stays up straight and lets his horse do the leaning.

Fig. 5.80. It is most important for horses to work over their hindquarters. This allows seven to eight feet of cow blocking range, as opposed to about three feet on a horse down low and turning on his front end.

Fig. 5.79. Dennis Murphy, a member of the U.S. Equestrian Jump Team, a former Foreman student. Straight up, he lets his horse lean.

Fig. 5.81. One of Foreman's first exhibition horses, War Paint, being rolled over his hocks by eight-year-old Gary Foreman. Note that the rider is standing and keeping his weight outside.

Fig. 5.82. When coming off a steep place on the side of a mountain, horse cavalries found that leaning forward in the security of the rider's groove allowed the horse to negotiate rough country more easily. Gary Foreman on world reining champion Paint, Warrior's Dream.

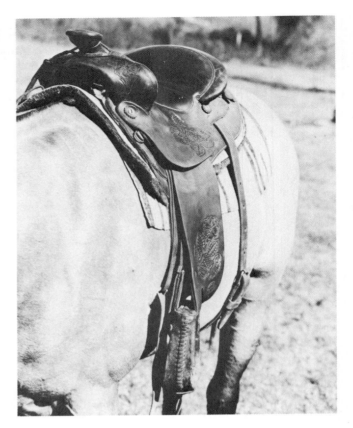

Fig. 5.83. All Balanced Ride Saddles have the same secure rideability because of the forward-hung stirrups and bulkless riggings in the rider's groove, where horses carry weight the best and are ridden the easiest. *A:* Side view.

Fig. 5.83*B:* Three-quarter front view.

6

The Rider

When you straddle your favorite horse, if you hope to achieve superb athletic performance, you must pay close attention to the movements of your hands and feet, your weight distribution, and your vocal commands. The horse is aware of all your actions, just as you would be if someone were riding on your shoulders. Your position and your actions, carefully controlled, aid in directing the horse's reactions.

🐎 THE RIDER'S POSITION

The rider's position affects the horse's physical ability to move efficiently. When turning at the gallop, sit straight up or lean slightly *away* from the desired turn. When turning hard to the right, place your weight slightly on the left and keep the upper body at a 90-degree angle to the ground. *Do not lean toward the turn.* This position can be observed in all the photographs of the move-basics. It is essential for good performance.

When traveling straight ahead, the rider can use his position to affect the horse's movements. The rider uses three basic positions: travel position, raised position and weight-back position *(figures 6.1 to 6.4).*

🐎 THE RIDER'S HANDS

In many respects the rider's hands are the extension of the rider's mind. They are the primary means by which most riders control their mounts. What the rider does with his hands controls the horse's head and therefore affects the horse's attitude. The horse not only feels the hand action through the bit but also can see what the hands are doing. The well-schooled rider uses all the senses of the horse to create a highly trained mount that responds to the "softest" signal possible. This is "finish" on the horse.

The way the reins are held influences the speed and ease with which the rider controls the horse. When guiding a horse, begin with both hands on the reins. After you have achieved lateral control, three fingers between the reins allows you to move in with the other hand to reinforce lateral control. Other systems of holding the reins are used depending on what is required. In the show ring only one finger is allowed between split reins. When a romal (California-style) is used— the entire hand is held around the reins with the reins coming from the bottom of the hand.

Fig. 6.2. *Raised position.* The rider is off her seat, with weight in the stirrups. This is the basic position, with only slight variations, for roping, jumping, stopping, hitting the ball in polo, racing, and lead changing. Becky Fuchs, Girls Rodeo Association world champion team roper and accredited Foreman instructor, on Quarter's Sissy.

Fig. 6.1. *Travel position.* This is the way a rider should sit a horse when traveling slowly, as in equitation classes. Both horse and rider are relaxed.

🐎 MOVE-WITH-HANDS

This move is among the more difficult skills to acquire. When a horse walks or gallops, he moves his head in a specific manner. Nature designed the horse in such a way that head motion is necessary for maximum efficiency. Head motion is especially important to the horse when agility at the gallop is needed. If the motion is restricted by the rider by holding steady pressure on the reins, the balance of the horse is affected.

When riding a horse at the gallop, feel the action of the saddle horn by placing your hands on it. This back-and-forth action is similar to and coordinates with the horse's head action.

Now lift your hands, while keeping light contact with the bit, and move them in the same rhythm that you felt on the saddle horn. A snaffle nonleverage bit should be used to learn the feel of the horse's head.

The less training a horse has received, the easier it is to feel the normal head motion. Riders who are unfamiliar with the move-with-hands train horses not to move their heads, thereby decreasing the proficiency of the animals. Whenever a horse is turned, regardless of the degree, the rider should work with the head action.

The horse sees and feels what the rider does with his hands. If the rider learns to use his hands as a cue (signal), it becomes possible to control the horse with less pressure on the bit.

Fig. 6.3. During stops the rider should be in the raised position, which makes it easier for the horse to bring his hind legs up and under him. This three-year-old filly, Two-D-Four, photographed during training, was the winner of the 1978 year-end high-point award in the Colorado Palomino Horse Breeders Association for all-age reining and was the Palomino Horse Breeders Association national junior reining champion. Trained and shown by Susan Baker.

Fig. 6.4. *Weight-back position.* This position is taken for slowing a horse, holding a hind lead around a turn, making drop-to-trot lead changes, and tiring a "chargy" horse. After the horse gets his hind feet well under him in roll moves, the rider can sit back to help the horse come out in correct leads. Monte Foreman riding.

🐎 LATERAL CONTROL

Lateral control is the ability to turn the horse by pulling his head toward the direction of the turn. The horse, through training, learns to turn with minimum resistance. Lateral control allows the rider to teach the horse to turn without contradicting basic balance needs. This, like other move-basics, is taught progressively. Combining lateral control with gentle neck-rein pressure achieves coordinated rein action.

🐎 USE OF HANDS AND LEGS

The horse's awareness of the rider's hand and leg positions can be used to motivate reaction. Using the hands and legs to signal for a turn or stop or even combining the signals to mean a turn during a stop, the rider can use less pressure on the bit. The horse soon learns to respond to these signals if they are consistent.

The security of the rider when moving, especially at speed, has a great deal to do with the horse's performance. A rider who leans in, uses the hands to stay on, or flops his legs has problems gaining control over the horse. If the rider must use his hands for balance, he cannot effectively use them for controlling the horse.

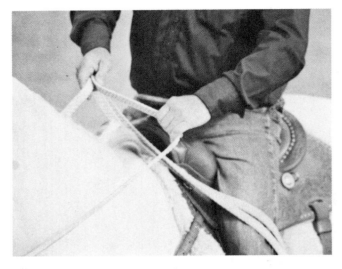

Fig. 6.5. When guiding a green colt, the rider needs both hands on the reins. To turn to the left, hold both reins in your right hand and slide your left hand down the rein as far as necessary to turn the horse laterally. Switch hands to turn to the right.

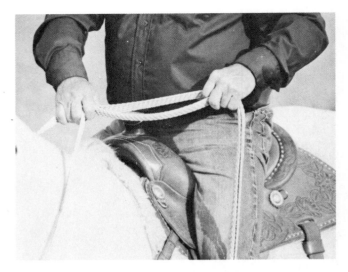

Fig. 6.6. After the horse will guide laterally, use three fingers between the reins. This allows lateral force to be applied effectively.

The same is true of careless movement of the upper body and legs. Through concentration and coaching, learn to ride astride a horse quietly, using both hands and legs to signal and guide the horse. There is no substitute for miles and wet saddle blankets. The rewards are more than worth the effort. 🐎

Fig. 6.7. A closer view of three fingers between the reins. Both reins come out between index finger and thumb, or the thumb may encircle the reins. This method is widely used in polo and was basic with the United States Cavalry.

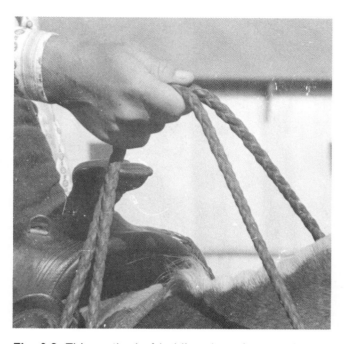

Fig. 6.8. This method of holding the reins, or with the index finger between them, is often used by western riders. The disadvantages are that it limits lateral control. Neck reining with force is ineffective.

Fig. 6.9. This way of holding the reins is widely used on the Pacific Coast. It also lacks lateral control, however, and handicaps guiding.

Fig. 6.10. This is the polo and military manner of holding four reins. For lateral control the nonleverage (snaffle) reins are the two outside reins; the two inside reins are leverage (curb) reins.

Fig. 6.11. This is the first step in reaching lateral control. The hand should be low and wide. Take hold of the horse's mouth and then pull until he gives. Do this from the ground first, if necessary.

LATERAL CONTROL

Fig. 6.12. In this sequence *(figs. 6.12–6.17)* Becky Fuchs, a Foreman Clinic instructor, is shown bending a green colt away from the fence. She goes down the rein with her left hand, pulling the horse's head left. This sequence is at the gallop; however, it is advisable to start at a walk, then a trot.

Fig. 6.13. The colt gives his head to the pull of the bit. The rider is in the slightly raised position, allowing the colt's hind feet to come forward. The rider's heels are down, with legs in the rider's groove, giving her maximum security.

Fig. 6.14. The colt continues to give his head. The rider is already beginning to use a coordinated rein action, turning with the leading rein (left rein) and neck-reining with the bearing rein (right rein).

Fig. 6.15. Now the rider does a rollaway toward the fence, and the same lateral-control basics are used. Note the security of the rider.

Fig. 6.16. The horse rolls away from the lead over his hocks. The rider continues to pull laterally while working with the horse's head action. Note the rider's straight-up position. *Never* lean in the direction you want to go.

Fig. 6.17. The horse is in perfect position to come out galloping in the right lead. Observe the natural action of the horse throughout the sequence. Now Becky sits, making sure that the colt comes out in the right lead.

Fig. 6.20. Two-D-Four responds to the rider's signals and pushes off for the next lifting stride.

Fig. 6.19. The rider lightly taps the horse with the rein ends on the right side where the neck joins the shoulder. This enforces the cue of the raised hand and the slight guiding effort—and Two-D-Four reacts.

Fig. 6.21. She pivots over the left hind leg with a galloping action. The rein hand continues suggesting the direction of turn. The subtle use of coordinated reins keeps the horse's head in good position.

Fig. 6.22. The rider uses his right leg on the girth as a cue to encourage more turning effort from the horse.

USE OF HANDS AND LEGS

Fig. 6.18. In this sequence *(figs. 6.18–6.23)* Monte Foreman is shown training Two-D-Four. Here he raises his rein hand and slightly guides the filly to begin turning over her hocks to the left. He holds the rein ends in his right hand to enforce the cue, if necessary.

Fig. 6.23. The rider continues a bumping action with his right leg on the horse's girth. Through the coordinated use of the rider's hands and legs, the horse learns to turn willingly and in rhythm.

Fig. 6.24. Becky and her heeling partner, Kathy Kennedy, reserve Girls Rodeo Association team-roping champion (on Quarter's Topsy), put the move-basics together.

Fig. 6.25. Becky Fuchs on Quarter's Topsy, Girls Rodeo Association Super Horse three years in a row, 1976 to 1978. The horse is owned, trained, and contested by Becky, GRA team-roping and steer-undecorating champion. The Super Horse title is based on annual money winnings.

7

The Turn on the Forehand

The **turn on the forehand** is primarily a training exercise to increase the sensitivity of the horse to leg cues when controlling the hindquarters. It is useful in opening gates and in ranch work, such as dragging heavy calves to the branding fire, when it provides a way to turn a horse to face the cattle without allowing slack in the rope. The turn on the forehand is a preparatory move-basic to teaching the side pass. It is important to use a nonleverage snaffle bit for both of these fundamentals during the learn-

ing phase. The horse pictured in *figures 7.1 to 7.4* is well trained, and a curb bit was used.

If the horse becomes confused, allow him to relax and then try again. Use no more force than necessary. When the horse rotates willingly around his front foot with a minimum of pressure, you are ready to teach side passing. The main goal is to teach the horse to respond to leg pressure by displacing his hindquarters away from that pressure.

TURN ON THE FOREHAND

Fig. 7.1. *The turn on the forehand.* In this sequence *(figs. 7.1–7.4)* the turn is to the left, around the horse's left front foot. Here the rider simultaneously puts pressure on the left rein, causing the horse's head to turn slightly to the left, and uses his left leg, well back, to motivate the horse to move his hindquarters to the right. Mike Foreman on Chappo Hancock. This horse starred in the American Quarter Horse Association film *Ride, Cowboy, Ride.*

Fig. 7.2. The rider increases the leg pressure, using a bumping action, if necessary. To prevent forward motion when the leg pressure is increased, he holds both sides of the horse's mouth to keep the left foreleg in the same place.

Fig. 7.3. The rider releases the leg pressure when the horse responds. This is his reward for moving away from the pressure.

Fig. 7.4. The rider repeats the leg pressure to get another step. The rider should strive for a series of turning steps in rhythm with the leg cue.

8

The Side Pass

The **side pass,** along with the turn on the forehand, teaches response to leg pressure for control of the hindquarters. This move-basic is essential to teach a horse collected lead changes. It is useful in opening gates, positioning rope horses in roping boxes, or getting your Coke off a corral post, as well as for general control.

Two ways are used to teach the horse and rider to side-pass. First, turn the horse on the forehand to the right. Then, as the horse willingly moves his hindquarters left, coordinate your rein action to cause the forequarters to move sideways to the left. This continuous movement causes the horse to side-pass with ease. If the horse becomes confused, stop the side-pass effort and make the horse turn on the forehand to the right. When the horse willingly moves his hindquarters again to the left, bring the coordinated rein action into play until a few side-passing steps to the left are accomplished. Use a press-and-release action.

The second method of teaching the side pass begins by walking a horse parallel to something like an arena fence (*not* a barbwire fence). The fence should be to your right. Stay about six to ten feet from the fence. Slightly collect the horse with mild pressure on both reins. Going to your left, use the right lower leg well back, just as you did in the turn on the forehand. Cause the horse to move his forequarters as seen in *figures 8.1 to 8.3.* When the horse responds by moving sideways, release your leg pressure to reward him. Apply pressure again to motivate another step, while coordinating the rein pressure in rhythm with your leg cue. After a few steps sideways, release the horse and allow him to walk out straight. This will help keep him calm. If the horse becomes excited or confused, allow him to walk out and relax and then try again. Do *not* overwork the horse.

Do not attempt to move the horse at a 90-degree angle, but keep the forequarters slightly in the lead. This forward angle gives the horse space to move and keeps him from stepping on his own feet. Practice regularly until the horse will side-pass with only light cues. Practice moving toward fences and gates. When you and the horse are accomplished at this move during the walk, you can gradually speed up the rhythm to a slow trot.

SIDE PASS

Fig. 8.1. *The side pass.* In this sequence *(figs. 8.1–8.3)* the horse moves to the left, crossing his right front foot in front of the left. Using coordinated rein action, the rider controls the movement of the forequarters. The rider's right leg presses by the rear girth to cause the horse to move his hindquarters to the left. Leg pressure is intermittent, exactly the same as in turn on the forehand. Monte Foreman on Barred's Ghost.

Fig. 8.2. The right hind foot of the horse passes in front of the left. The horse moves sideways and slightly forward at a walk. The rider restrains the horse's head a little with coordinated rein.

Fig. 8.3. Note the continuation of the rhythmic movement, as the right front foot passes in front of the left.

9

Leads

The sequence photographs in this book were taken at four pictures per second. That is not fast enough to separate each step of a galloping horse. Therefore, to explain leads, sketches made from 16-mm. films shot at 64 frames a second have been used (these sketches originally appeared in Foreman's book *Cantankerous Leads*).

A horse can gallop four different ways, two in rhythm and two out of rhythm. If the horse is out of rhythm, his agility is severely limited. The rider must always know by feel which lead the horse is in and know how to cause the horse to move into the correct lead. Without a thorough understanding of leads, the rider handicaps the horse and his performance.

·First, it is necessary to understand exactly what a *lead* is *(see figures 9.1 to 9.11)*. The canted angle of the horse while galloping is easily observed by a spectator. In a good stop this angle should stay the same until the stop is completed. Owing to the canted angle of the horse's body when he is galloping, the rider can feel his knee on the leading side traveling ahead of the knee on the following side. If the horse is in the left lead, your left knee is traveling ahead of your right knee. Your leg, hip, and upper body will travel farther ahead on the lead side. That is how you feel the lead.

Follow the left-lead movement through the drawings in *figures 9.3 to 9.11*. The dark leg wraps are on the leading legs. Observe the way each leg works. The horse's body always moves sideways from the following side to the leading side during each stride.

What about the hind lead? This must be felt with the rider's seat. If the horse is smooth, then the rear lead is correct. If the ride feels as though your rear shocks are broken on a washboard road, then the horse is in the wrong lead behind. This is called "disunited," "cross-firing," or "cow loping." Learn to *feel* both front and rear leads. The expert rider feels it as if the horse were an extension of the rider's body. When a horse changes leads, he changes the "cant" of his body and footwork. That is why leads are so important.

The *wrong-lead turn* shown in *figures 9.12 to 9.24* demonstrates the importance of leads, since this is a dangerously limiting factor when a horse turns. If it were impossible for the horse to turn awkwardly, it would be unnecessary for you to know how it happens and what to do to prevent or correct it. Riders frequently turn their mounts toward the wrong lead, often through ignorance but sometimes intentionally. Making a wrong-lead turn intentionally can be a training technique to polish lead control in the finishing stages of training. This is known as a *counter canter* or *false lead*. At times you may want to turn slightly away from the lead while going slow. To be accurate in horse handling, however, the rider must always know what lead the horse is in.

To understand the lead limitations of the horse galloping in the wrong lead, carefully follow the horse's leg action in *figures 9.12 to 9.24*. Again, the leading legs are wearing dark leg wraps.

While he is in a wrong lead, the horse is physically unable to do a quick, efficient turn. The more force the rider applies, the harder it is for the horse to turn with agility. In the correct lead, however, the horse is balanced for the turn with maximum agility. All move-basics relate to this fundamental rule of natural science.

A *disunited turn* occurs when a horse galloping with the hind lead not matching the front lead attempts to turn. The unmatched leads diminish his agility and also create a very uncomfortable gallop. If the horse turns when he is sharply disunited, the move is not as dangerous as a wrong-lead turn, but the efficiency of the horse is greatly reduced. Without the hind leg properly under the body, the horse cannot pivot well or drive forward effectively. A disunited turn to the left is illustrated in *figures 9.25 to 9.37*. The horse is on the left lead in front, the right lead behind. The dark leg wraps are on the leading left front leg and the disunited nonleading left hind leg.

To correct a wrong hind lead, the rider has several options. The horse may be dropped to a trot and started in the correct lead at the gallop, as described further in chapter 11. By speeding up the horse's gallop and standing in the stirrups, leaning slightly *away* from the lead, you can enable an agile horse to catch his proper hind lead. Also motivate the horse to get his hindquarters back in line by using your leg, a bat, or long rein ends on the *opposite side* of the desired lead. To correct a wrong front lead, simply rein the horse slightly toward the desired lead.

As you can see in these drawings and by observing all galloping move-basics, knowledge of leads is essential. A good horse will try to move efficiently, but an unschooled rider can severely handicap his mount. Remember, always lean *away* from the lead you want. 🐎

WHAT IS A LEAD?

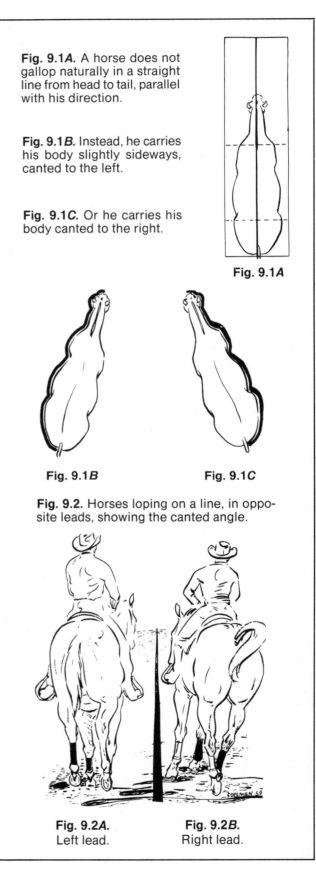

Fig. 9.1A. A horse does not gallop naturally in a straight line from head to tail, parallel with his direction.

Fig. 9.1B. Instead, he carries his body slightly sideways, canted to the left.

Fig. 9.1C. Or he carries his body canted to the right.

Fig. 9.1A

Fig. 9.1B   Fig. 9.1C

Fig. 9.2. Horses loping on a line, in opposite leads, showing the canted angle.

Fig. 9.2A. Left lead.   **Fig. 9.2B.** Right lead.

LEFT-LEAD GALLOP

Fig. 9.3. Left front leg out, three hooves on the ground.

Fig. 9.4. The right front leg is helped by the left hind leg.

Fig. 9.5. The weight shifts toward the left front, two hooves down.

Fig. 9.6. Three feet off, all the weight on the left front.

Fig. 9.7. The right hind leg makes a short stride forward to the vicinity of the stifle joint.

Fig. 9.8. The left hind leg makes a long stride forward, the left front off the ground.

Fig. 9.9. The left hind leg goes well forward into the vicinity of the rear girth.

Fig. 9.10. The left lead is easy to recognize in *figs. 9.3, 9.4,* and *9.8–11.*

Fig. 9.11. The left front and hind legs always reach ahead more than the other legs at the left lead.

WRONG-LEAD LEFT TURN

Fig. 9.12. Watch the weight-carrying leg in this sequence, which shows why it is so difficult for a horse to turn left when he is traveling on the right lead.

Fig. 9.13. As the horse's body moves left to right on the right lead, he must continue to do so on left turns. The front leg turning push is missing here.

Fig. 9.14. While the horse is on the leading front leg, the left hind leg moves to the right, *away* from the direction of the turn.

Fig. 9.15. The left front leg crosses to the outside. It is easy for the horse to fall if the hoof slips when weight goes on it.

Fig. 9.16. The right hind leg makes an extrawide step to the outside, away from the direction of turn. His body leans excessively, and his legs won't stay under him.

Fig. 9.17. There is no pivot leg under the horse's rear quarters.

Fig. 9.18. The body rocks sideways left to right, instead of right to left as in the correct lead turn.

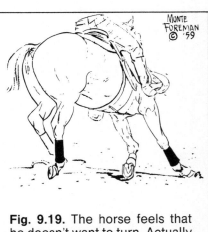

Fig. 9.19. The horse feels that he doesn't want to turn. Actually he can't turn, because nature restricts his movements.

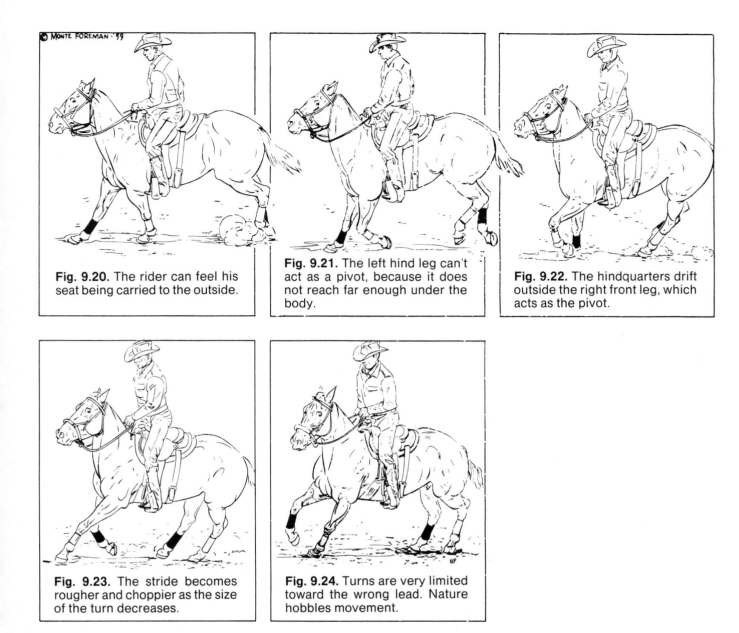

Fig. 9.20. The rider can feel his seat being carried to the outside.

Fig. 9.21. The left hind leg can't act as a pivot, because it does not reach far enough under the body.

Fig. 9.22. The hindquarters drift outside the right front leg, which acts as the pivot.

Fig. 9.23. The stride becomes rougher and choppier as the size of the turn decreases.

Fig. 9.24. Turns are very limited toward the wrong lead. Nature hobbles movement.

DISUNITED TURN

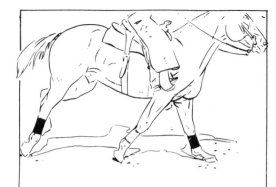

Fig. 9.25. The horse is on the left lead with the front legs but on the right lead with the hind legs.

Fig. 9.26. The front legs are on the correct lead for best turnability, but the hind legs are on the wrong lead.

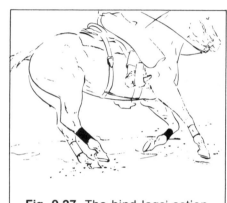

Fig. 9.27. The hind legs' action carries the hindquarters away from the direction of the turn. Look at the left hind leg in *fig. 9.26* and note how wide it is tracking.

Fig. 9.28. Look at the right hind leg in *figs. 9.26–9.28* and note the awkward wide step outside, just as on wrong-lead turns.

Fig. 9.29. The left front leg crosses, causing it to come down with too much weight on it.

Fig. 9.30. Of course, as seen here, the front legs must do more turning than the hind legs.

Fig. 9.31. Where is that pivoting and weight-carrying hind leg? The wrong hind lead does not have the hind-leg pivot.

Fig. 9.32. With no weight supporting him, most of the horse's weight must go onto the leading leg, and it must turn him too.

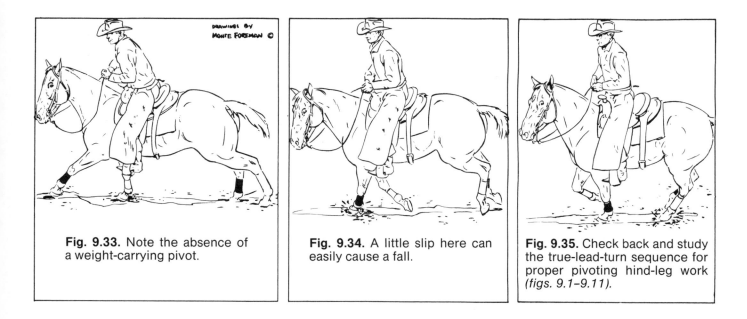

Fig. 9.33. Note the absence of a weight-carrying pivot.

Fig. 9.34. A little slip here can easily cause a fall.

Fig. 9.35. Check back and study the true-lead-turn sequence for proper pivoting hind-leg work *(figs. 9.1–9.11).*

Fig. 9.36. The forequarters' turning ability is restricted by the hindquarters' movement away from the direction of the turn.

Fig. 9.37. The rider can feel his seat being carried wide, and there is always a rough bumping action in the horse's gallop.

10

Posting at the Trot and the Natural Depart to the Correct Lead

This chapter combines posting at the trot and the natural depart to the correct lead. The same sequence of photographs is used to illustrate both move-basics. These moves are combined here because the rider who can feel the natural rhythm of the horse and work in accord with it is more effective in all aspects of lead selection.

🐎 POSTING AT THE TROT

Posting at the trot is the movement of the rider rising and sitting rhythmically in the saddle. The rising action is forward and up *(figure 10.2).* Posting at the trot has been done by riders for many years. From the days of the horse soldier to modern days trail riders have found the movement easier for the horse and rider. Posting is a standard of English riding.

Posting on the correct diagonal is moving in rhythm with a particular front foot. If the horse is moving to the right in the arena, the rider rises in rhythm with the left front foot. The foot is harder to see than the point of the shoulder. Since the shoulder works in time with the foot, watch the point of the shoulder. As it moves ahead, rise smoothly with it.

The value of this move-basic to the rider is substantial. First, it teaches the rider to work with the horse's rhythm. Second, it is much easier for the horse to take the desired lead at the gallop. When the rider can post on either diagonal by looking at the shoulder, he must then learn to do it by feel. Try to grow beyond using a visual check and learn to *feel* the horse's muscular movements, but don't be afraid to take a glance to be sure you are posting correctly.

When the horse is circling to the right, the rider rises as the left front foot of the horse moves up *(figure 10.2).* The rider then sits as the left front foot lands on the ground. The rider prepares to rise again as the left front foot comes off the ground *(figure 10.3).*

To be in harmony with the horse, the rider must feel the rhythm of the horse's movements. This begins at the trot. Discipline your efforts and learn to post equally well on either front foot. Know this movement so well that you can shut your eyes and feel the action of the horse's front feet.

🐎 NATURAL DEPART TO THE CORRECT LEAD

This method is easiest for horse and rider to learn. There are two other, more difficult methods of getting the desired lead: the rollaway to

POSTING

Fig. 10.1. The horse is trotting in a large circle to the right *(figs. 10.1–10.6).* Note the running martingale and the adaptation of the Foreman bit. Here the reins are attached to the nonleverage snaffle ring on the bit. This allows better lateral control of the horse. The rider is coming down in the saddle as the left front foot comes down.

Fig. 10.2. The horse continues to circle. The rider rises with the left front foot. This is the correct posting rhythm when asking for the right lead. This posting action makes it easier for the horse to impulse, or move, into the desired lead. The easier it is for a horse to perform a move, the less force is required.

Fig. 10.3. As the horse's left front foot comes off the ground, the rider impulses the horse to extend to the gallop by clucking, then bumping with his left leg back by the rear girth. A flat bat or the ends of long reins can be used on the horse's left hip to enforce the leg cue.

the correct lead and the collected depart to the correct lead, the latter being the more difficult. The natural depart requires less training and less force than the others. It is the instinctive way a horse moves from a trot to a gallop. Since it is a natural move, the horse remains relaxed because it is easy for him.

The lead selection is made possible by turning a horse in a large circle. As the horse circles, the rider *impulses,* or moves, the horse in a specific manner. The natural depart to the lead should be the first way a horse is trained to carry the rider into the gallop. It can be used throughout the useful life of the horse to

Fig. 10.4. The horse prepares to extend from a trot to a gallop. The easy turn to the right is continued. The rider is sitting as the right front foot is about to come to the ground. The rider's body should remain straight up, *never* leaning toward the desired lead.

Fig. 10.5. The horse gallops into the right lead as the gentle turn continues.

Fig. 10.6. Throughout this move-basic the horse is gradually turned to the right. The leg cue is back and on the *off*-lead side. The rider stays straight up to the ground or slightly to the *off*-lead side. Any enforcement of the leg cue is on the left side. All guiding with the reins is lateral. Neck reining with force should not be applied. Be sure the horse turns his head slightly *toward* the direction of travel. When the rider asks for a right lead, the horse's head should be slightly to the right. The horse in this sequence, Bender Bar, was trained by Monte Foreman. Under Guy Gauthier, a Foreman student, he won the Canadian National Amateur Reining Championship—six weeks after these photographs were made.

get the correct lead. Refinement of this move-basic makes it useful in the show ring. Of all methods of taking the correct lead, this one creates the least amount of stress.

It is essential in training to be able to select a desired lead when asking a horse to gallop. The natural depart to the lead allows you to move your horse from trot to gallop very early in training.

Working a horse rhythmically is at the heart of all galloping move-basics. The horse sets the beat in relation to the speed of the gallop. The rider must be in harmony with that beat. 🐎

11

The Drop-to-Trot Lead Change

The **drop-to-trot lead change** is the foundation of all advanced move-basics. On the surface this maneuver seems simple and unexciting; however, further observation shows that all reactions of horse and rider come into play when this move is executed efficiently. This move-basic is the only way a green horse can change leads slowly. No matter what degree of finish is achieved on a horse, the drop-to-trot lead change remains useful and essential.

To perform a drop-to-trot lead change, the horse must be allowed to turn his head freely and react to light leg cues. This move-basic is used in training the horse to respond to lateral bit pressure, especially at the gallop. It also demands rider accuracy in guiding the horse and is the best maneuver to perfect the use of hands, legs, and body position.

This maneuver should be used in everyday work with the horse. Use it when warming up the horse to relieve tension or overreaction to cues. Performed correctly, the drop-to-trot lead change is one of the better ways to re-train a "chargy" horse.

Figures 11.1 to 11.5 show through sequence photographs a drop-to-trot lead change on a well-schooled horse using a short-shank Foreman bit. On a green colt a nonleverage snaffle bit and a running martingale are used for the maneuver. At first the rider should cause the horse to break from a gallop to a trot by turning the horse toward the old lead to a much larger degree than that illustrated here. The greener the horse, the more turn is involved. The rider must lean well back over the loin and allow a long reaction time by the green horse or colt. Any unschooled horse needs more turn, very little pull-back on the reins, and a lot of time to react. If the horse does not drop smoothly to the trot with the first turning effort, continue to turn smoothly until he trots. Circle at the trot until everything is ready; then turn toward the new lead, continuing the circling turn and ask for the new lead as in the natural depart to correct lead.

Variations must be used to prevent anticipation of the lead change. The horse should not be patterned to the point that he anticipates the new lead. To prevent anticipation of lead change, drop to a trot and take the same lead out. By using variations as the rider sees fit, the horse will continue to make smooth transitions from gallop to trot to gallop in the new lead *(see figures 11.6 to 11.9).*

To be effective, a drop-to-trot lead change must be done smoothly. Concentrate on lateral flexion. The horse and rider never outgrow the usefulness of this working move-basic. 🐎

DROP-TO-TROT LEAD CHANGE

Fig. 11.1. *The drop-to-trot lead change (figs. 11.1–11.5).* Here the horse is galloping in the right lead. The rider increases the horse's turn toward the right. Monte Foreman riding Barred's Ghost.

Fig. 11.2. The rider leans back, which helps the horse drop to a trot.

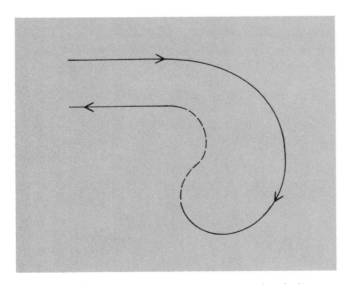

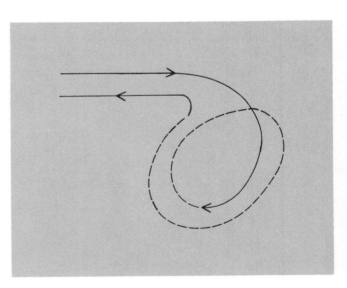

Fig. 11.6. The pattern for the drop-to-trot lead change. The arrows show the direction of travel; the broken line is the trot.

Fig. 11.7. Out the new-lead pattern.

Fig. 11.3. The horse has dropped to a trot. The rider prepares to cue the horse to take the new lead to the left by bringing his right leg back near the rear girth. This also aids the horse in dropping to a trot.

Fig. 11.4. The horse is now turning left, rolling up on his new lead foot. The rider must turn the horse's head toward the new lead. He impulses the horse at this point by posting with the right front foot, pressing the horse, well back, with his right leg. A flat bat or long rein end may be used on the horse's right hip to enforce the leg cue, if necessary.

Fig. 11.5. The move-basic has been completed. The horse is galloping in the new lead, relaxed and smooth. Note the horse's head position, turned slightly to the left lead.

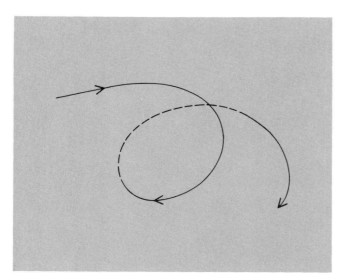

Fig. 11.8. Out the same-lead pattern.

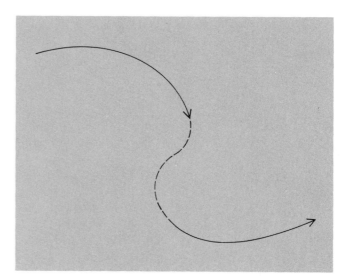

Fig. 11.9. The line of travel, as *figs. 11.1–11.5* illustrate.

12

The Natural Flying Lead Change

The front-foot-first lead change is the most natural way a horse changes leads without interference or collection by the rider. This technology was discovered, proved, and named by Foreman in 1943 and documented in 1946 in "Horse Handling Science," a series of articles for *Texas Cattleman Magazine,* later published in booklet form.

When he is being ridden, it is not a natural action for a galloping horse to maintain agility when changing direction. He changes leads easily in his front legs, but he has difficulty changing leads in the hind legs. Virtually everything that riders do naturally (or are taught to accept as "correct") causes a horse's hind legs to "hang up" and remain disunited.

It is much easier for a horse to change both leads if the rider stands, instead of sitting, during the maneuver. The rider must also lean *away* from the direction of the turn—and turn a little "extra" to the lead the horse is on *before asking for the change.* Do not turn, and particularly do not neck-rein, toward the new lead. Lay your leg against the horse's side and straighten him out. When you feel him change, then, and only then, do you turn to the new direction. The horse must be running when he changes leads—the faster he goes, the easier the changes. In more than 1,500 Foreman Clinics more than 75,000 riders have changed

leads in this way during the fifth hour of riding instruction.

The example of a natural flying lead change shown in *figures 12.1 to 12.9* starts with the horse in the right lead (the dark leg bandages indicate the lead the horse is on throughout the maneuver). In figure 12.4 the horse is airborne in the midst of the change, so there is no lead. This maneuver is done on a straight-line diagonal across the arena *(see figure 12.10A).*

Photoanalysis has shown that the horse must be in the correct lead before turning to be efficient. The method described here teaches the horse to change leads with a combination of leg cues and gentle guidance with the bit. Most horses must be at a medium gallop to perform this change smoothly. There are rare horses that are very athletic and can change leads at a slow gallop. However, training techniques should be designed for the average student and horse, while allowing rapid progress for the exceptionally talented.

When the horse is well schooled at faster speeds, slow down until you find the slowest speed possible for "clean" lead changes. The rider's proficiency will have a lot to do with the minimum speed attainable.

Before 1945 the only flying lead change known and documented was the collected

NATURAL FLYING LEAD CHANGE

Fig. 12.1. Here the horse is galloping at a medium speed in the right lead, as the legs in dark bandages indicate. As the horse approaches the center of the arena, the rider smoothly rises in the saddle and leans slightly to the right, his right leg pushed well back to cue the lead change.

Fig. 12.2. The horse's right front foot has landed, and the lead change begins.

Fig. 12.3. The rider guides the horse with a minimum amount of pressure on the bit toward the direction of the new lead. Be careful not to tip the horse's nose to the right, for this will cause awkwardness.

Fig. 12.4. As the horse's four feet become airborne, he changes rhythm with his front feet. The horse is motivated by the approaching turn, and the leg cue of the rider pushing the horse left.

Fig. 12.5. The front lead has now changed.

Fig. 12.6. The horse lands on the right front foot and rolls up on his lead left front foot.

Fig. 12.7. The left front foot is now the leading leg. The rider must not sit down until the hind lead change is completed. To do so will hinder the action of the hindquarters and can cause the horse to make an incomplete change.

Fig. 12.8. This stride changes the hind lead foot.

Fig. 12.9. The change is now completed. Never lean toward the new lead or neck-rein with force to get the horse to change leads.

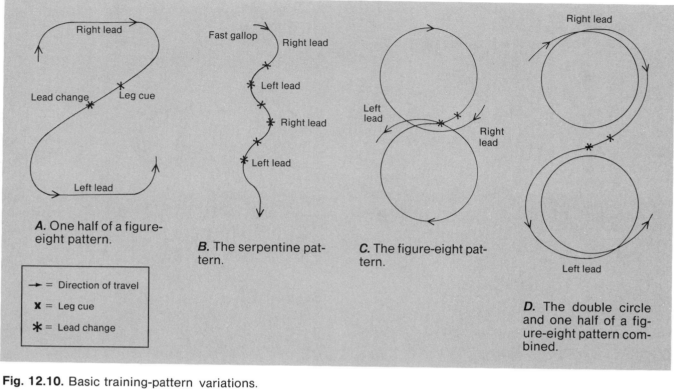

A. One half of a figure-eight pattern.

B. The serpentine pattern.

C. The figure-eight pattern.

→ = Direction of travel

x = Leg cue

∗ = Lead change

D. The double circle and one half of a figure-eight pattern combined.

Fig. 12.10. Basic training-pattern variations.

change. Even today some dressage experts claim that one should collect, impulse, and side-pass a horse for at least two years before allowing him to try his first flying lead change. Eighty-five percent of the horses trained by the Foreman method can do natural flying lead changes within the first week of handling.

Several variations in the riding pattern are used to increase the agility of the horse and to sharpen the horse-and-rider team for speed events requiring lead changes, such as barrel racing, stake racing, pole bending, jumping, and polo. Variations are also essential to prevent anticipation of the lead change *(see figure 12.10B–D).*

Collected lead changes are useful in competitive events that require a slow canter with a change of leads in the air. All flying changes are too difficult for unpracticed eyes to analyze or identify, but in Foreman films, in slow motion, it is no problem.

Before the collected dressage hind-feet-first change is attempted, your horse should be able to side-pass easily while moving slightly forward, at a walk, slow trot, and canter in each lead. The horse's face should be carried perpendicular to the ground, directed by the rider's "synchronized hands movement."

When this is accomplished, the rider must work to displace the horse's hindquarters sideways, using leg, leanaway body, and reins. Use your leg pressure well back on the leading side to force the horse's hindquarters over. Slightly "gallop" your hands as you turn the horse's body away from the new lead desired. Only through slow-motion photoanalysis can this entire sequence of events be clearly shown and demonstrated. With your "synchronized hands movement," slow and collect your horse for a couple of strides, and then gradually ask for his hindquarter change to the new lead. The combined "aids" of turning the horse's

COLLECTED LEAD CHANGE

Fig. 12.11. *A collected lead change (figs. 12.11–12.13).* Note the degree of collection. The face of the horse is 90 degrees to the ground. Any additional flexion would be considered overbreaking at the poll. The rider has her weight forward, allowing the horse to lift his hind legs and change lead behind with less effort. She brings her right leg well back, cueing the horse to move his hindquarter to the left in the direction of the new lead. Susan Baker riding Barred's Ghost during the Colorado State Fair. This change was videotaped for use in clinics and seminars on judging.

body away from the new lead and the "impulsing slow down" make the horse change his hind feet before his front feet. Sometimes, but not often, a horse changes behind but not in front. Guide slightly toward the new lead to change his front lead if necessary.

In *figures 12.11 to 12.13,* Susan Baker, on one of Monte Foreman's clinic exhibition horses, Barred's Ghost, sets an example of a western riding pattern doing "dressage" hind-foot-first lead changes. On exceptionally agile horses side-pass front-foot-first lead changes can be done with equal effectiveness. 🐎

Fig. 12.12. The horse is ready to roll up on his leading right front foot then both hind feet become airborne. The right hind foot goes to the ground first. The left hind foot reaches farther forward, and the horse has changed leads hind feet going to the ground first. While he is in the air, he changes his front lead.

Fig. 12.13. The right front foot has gone to the ground. The horse reaches farther forward with his left foot, which is now his leading front foot. This change has occurred in less than one third of a second.

13

Balanced Stops

Balanced stops are discussed before roll moves so that the reader can better understand the methods of motivating the horse to react with minimum effort. In teaching students and training horses, however, the rollaway from the lead is taught before the straight stop. Experience has shown that first rolling the horse 180 degrees with very little straight stopping gives better results.

The following method of stopping a horse has been carefully researched. Many years of riding, traveling, and teaching led to the development of the method. Countless still photographs and yards of motion pictures carefully document how a horse stops. To do an analytical study and design a method of teaching, Foreman first had to select a model. For years the calf-roping horse has made the rodeo cowboy's living with his efficient stops. Therefore, Foreman went to the National Finals Rodeo to photograph the cream of the crop performing stops. In no other competitive field are the demands on the horse's stop so great. The horse-and-rider team compete for one year against hundreds of other ropers, and only the top fifteen qualify for the National Finals. The test is against the stopwatch, not an individual's opinion. The stop of the horse has a lot to do with the reading on that stopwatch. An out-of-balance stop gives a jolt, making it difficult for the rider to get off smoothly and handle the

calf with the horse backing quickly. Nowhere else in the world is a horse's stop tested so thoroughly.

In 1946, Foreman began a photoanalysis study to discover how and why these calf-roping horses stop so efficiently. The first thing he observed was that the human eye records very little of what a horse does in a ten-second run. This chapter tells the rest of the story and shows how these principles can be applied in training riding horses.

The fundamentals of the balanced stop are also used by horse and rider in all move-basics, such as the 180-degree roll, that require the horse to move his hindquarters into the stop position. The same cue, the same rider position, and the same reaction of the horse can be observed in all these move-basics. It is essential that the rider have a comprehensive understanding of these fundamentals.

🐎 COMPONENTS OF THE BALANCED STOP

An analysis of the calf-roping horse below will be paralleled with the balanced stop of a riding horse. The comparison will apply directly to the young rope horse. With the polished professional rope horse the stop action is so keen that it is difficult to separate the components.

The Cue to Stop

This is the preparatory command.

The Calf Horse. As the horse moves into roping position behind the calf, he anticipates stopping. The horse slows, rates the calf, and mentally prepares to stop. He is "loaded" for the stop.

The Riding Horse. With no calf to provide a cue, the rider must softly tell the horse "Whoaa." The horse associates the voice command with stopping. The mental reaction is set in gear, and he also becomes "loaded" for the stop.

The Trigger

This is the command for execution.

The Calf Horse. The roper, well forward in the saddle, throws the rope, jerks the slack, and steps off. The proficient roper does this smoothly and very quickly. This pulls the trigger in the mind of the horse. He has put his stop muscles into action.

The Riding Horse. Without a rope and with no intention of getting off the horse, the rider must use other signals to trigger the horse to stop. Experience has shown that a slow forward motion of the rein as seen in *figures 13.7 to 13.10* works well for most riders. The horse feels the reins go slack and sees the hand motion. This triggers the trained horse to put his stop muscles in action.

The Enforcement

It takes a lot of energy for a horse to stop when he is running wide open. Smart as he is, he would rather not do sudden stops if it were left up to him. To get that powerful balanced stop you want, there must be a threat hanging over the horse.

The Calf Horse. Most calf horses are ridden with a leverage bit or a leverage hackamore. A tie-down adjusted on the short side is also the usual rule. When stopping, the horse feels the tie-down as he raises his head, and from experience he knows that the roper can give a pull on the bit if the need arises. The jerk of the calf also enforces the stop. If the horse is in balance with his hind feet well under his body, he can absorb the jerk readily.

The Riding Horse. Without stepping off, which is a very strong signal to the horse, or a calf threatening a hard jerk on the rope, other ways of motivating Dobbin to get his tail in the ground must be used. A gentle pull and release on the bit is most effective. The pulls increase in force if the horse fails to react strongly. Always start with gentle pulls in rhythm with the off-lead front foot.

The actions and reactions described and illustrated here are those of a trained horse and rider. Refresh yourself on the principles of how a horse learns *(chapter 3)* for a better understanding of the training process.

🐎 KEYS TO THE BALANCED STOP

All Foreman training methods were initiated to allow the horse to use his natural agility to the fullest. The easier it is for the horse, the quicker he learns. In training a horse to stop in balance, the keys to consistency are rider position on the horse, allowance for the horse's reaction time, the three-stride factor, the lead factor, and the horse's head position.

Rider Position

The good calf roper is forward on his horse from the start of the run until he steps to the ground. Years ago many ropers would fall back in the saddle, pull hard on the horse, and then step off. Of course, roping times were much slower. The forward position is essential during the stop, as the photos in this chapter show clearly. Only when the weight of the rider is off the horse's loin can the horse easily thrust his hind feet well under his body.

Reaction Time

In the early stages of training at least three or four strides should be allowed between the cue and the first easy pull on the bit. This delay is essential. As the horse becomes conditioned to the cue, he will react as quickly as he can. Then the rider works with this reaction time. As with trained athletes, the horse's reaction time shortens with practice. Time to react is always needed and must not be ignored.

The Three-Stride Factor

A Volkswagen bug traveling 20 miles per hour on dry pavement takes approximately 50 feet to stop. This includes a driver reaction time of ¾ second, according to the National Highway Safety Council. A horse traveling at 20 miles per hour is no different from other objects in motion. It takes time and distance to bring the horse to a complete stop. And remember, a horse does not have power brakes and radial tires.

Most of the problems that arise in stopping a running horse result from trying to get the horse sliding too soon. On average ground the horse needs to reset his hind feet at least twice before attempting to slide or hold. Hard-running roping horses get down in balance usually in three strides, rarely less. On slick ground a horse can hold earlier. On sticky ground it may take more than three strides for the horse to reduce his speed and be able to keep his hind feet locked in stop position. The first two strides of a balanced stop are almost imperceptible to the untrained eye. The last

stride dominates the perceived image, since it lasts the longest. Only through Foreman photoanalysis was this principle discovered.

Lead Factor

The importance of leads in the stop has long been overlooked. Multitudes of photographs have been published of calf-roping horses stopping. In these photos you can observe that most of the horses stop in a canted position. The cant, or angle, of the horse's body is a natural factor in a well-balanced stop. A stop in balance is a galloping maneuver; therefore, leads are as important in stops as they are in all galloping moves. The horse should remain in the same lead throughout the stop. When leads are switched during the stop—for example, in the second stride—propping of the front legs and poorer holds often result.

Head Position

A top calf roper leaves his horse's head alone throughout the stop. The horse reacts to a specific sequence of events that has been repeated time after time. Because the horse's head is left alone, he can balance efficiently. If any pull on the bit is made, it should be made when the horse is almost stopped.

The horse needs maximum use of his head to balance. In stopping a ridden horse without the strong motivation of calf roping, more use of the bit is required. The manner in which you use the bit determines the horse's head position throughout the stop. Leaning back and jerking the horse's head up throws the horse off balance. Start easy and allow for reaction time. The pulls on the bit should start with gentle give-and-take pressure. In the first few strides the bit is used as a signal. If the horse does not respond, the pull becomes harder.

Pull on the bit in rhythm with the off-lead front foot. As this foot strikes the ground, pull on the bit, then release and pull again in rhythm until the horse stops. This makes it easier for

BALANCED STOP ON CALF-ROPING HORSE

Fig. 13.1. *The balanced stop on the calf-roping horse (figs. 13.1–13.4).* The voice command "Whoaa" is given before any other cue. The horse is already reacting as the rider's rein hand goes to his neck for balance and the rider begins to step off. Pat Wyse demonstrating on his horse Chum.

Fig. 13.2. Efficient stops allow the rider to get off fast and in balance. The rider pushes back over the cantle preparing for the impact, weight on the stirrup. The horse has reaction time without interference. The rider concentrates on looking straight ahead, which prevents him from twisting his body. He keeps his belt buckle facing straight ahead. The horse is on his lead front foot, his hind feet are arcing for a longer stride. Foreman photoanalysis of the National Finals Rodeos shows that stopping this way allows an effective jerk on the calf, enables the horse to back up faster, and is easier for the roper to get down in balance and reach his calf in shape to win.

Fig. 13.3. This is not a propped stop, as is evidenced by the horse's left front foot, which is beginning to flex, and the leading front foot, which is extending to the ground. The rider is in excellent balance; his left foot is parallel to the horse's body, not "toeing" the horse. The rider is also in position to remain in the stirrup and school the horse by pulling on the reins if necessary. The rider should keep his body close to the horse throughout this maneuver.

Fig. 13.4. While tactfully schooling the horse with the reins to finish the stop, the rider is getting down in first-rate shape.

Fig. 13.5. This photograph demonstrates the similarity of stopping action on the ridden horse—the same rider, the same horse as shown in *figs. 13.1–13.4.* Note the raised position of the rider.

BALANCED STOP ON RIDING HORSE

Fig. 13.6. *The balanced stop on the riding horse (figs. 13.6–13.10).* Here the horse is in the right lead, and the rider's weight is raised. As in all roll moves and stops, the voice command "Whoaa" is given softly—the "Whoaa" occurs before any other action is taken. A "Whoaa, whoaa, whoaa" signal may also be used. Do not be loud or harsh. The horse hears very well—and so does a horse-show judge. Cues to the horse become a habit for the rider as well as for the horse. Monte Foreman demonstrates on his World Reining Champion Warrior's Dream.

Fig. 13.7. Allow for the horse's reaction time between the voice command and the hand signal. The horse is beginning to react to the voice cue as the rider signals for the stop with hand and rein. Make a brushing action starting at the wither and moving up the neck. Do not press hard on the horse's neck, and do not tip your shoulders forward. Allow for reaction time between the hand signal and the first easy pull on the bit. The greener the horse, the longer you must wait.

Fig. 13.8. The horse moves onto his lead right front foot as the hind feet prepare to thrust well under his body. In a split second it will be easiest for him to brake with his hind feet. The rider has pulled the bit gently in rhythm with the off-lead front foot. The pull is released as the lead foot strikes the ground. The horse has unrestricted head movement as he prepares to make the second checking effort in the stop. The rider's weight is raised in the stirrups.

Fig. 13.9. The horse can now, in the third stride of the stop, keep his hind feet in sliding position, under the front girth. The first two checking efforts slowed his speed enough to allow this. Observe how the right-front knee is flexed, preparing to move in a running motion as the hind feet slide.

Fig. 13.10. This is the balanced stop that the eye perceives. Very little is observed of the first two strides as recorded in *figs. 13.6–13.9.* These photographs were taken every one-quarter second. The entire stopping maneuver took a little over one second. Even with this stop-action photography the camera does not record everything that happens. No wonder there is so much misinformation about stops.

CALF-ROPING STOP

Fig. 13.11. *A calf-roping stop (figs. 13.11–13.15).* This is the first checking stride in the three strides of the stop. The horse is reacting to a well-honed conditioned reflex. The rider's balance is up and forward. Note the position of his left hand and the slack in the rein.

Fig. 13.12. The horse, in the second stopping stride, continues to take off additional speed in preparation for the third and final stopping effort. The rider continues his smooth step off. No pull on the bit occurs throughout the sequence.

the horse to stop in balance. Stopping a horse is one of the more difficult techniques to learn, but it is learnable. Once mastered, it must be continually practiced. You will then be able to improve the stop on any horse.

Guiding the horse very slightly toward the lead prevents undesired lead changes in the stop. The same-lead roll, discussed in chapter 16, is a fundamental exercise during training to improve the stop and keep the horse keen in his balanced efforts.

🐎 REINFORCEMENT

Refer to chapter 3 to refresh your understanding of conditioned reflex. The prime reason why a calf-roping horse learns to stop well is consistency of the roper's signals when he catches the calf. Rarely do you see a good calf-roping horse stay keen under a poor roper. The erratic actions of a learning roper only confuse the horse. There is no opportunity for the horse to learn a conditioned reflex if the signals change each time out of the box.

The same principle applies to the riding horse. The sequence of signals, allowance for reaction time, and enforcement must be precise. *Consistency* separates the expert from the intermediate.

Whether you rope a calf, step off, or stay in the saddle, the same basics are followed: preparatory command, reaction time, and enforcement, if necessary. The step-off sequence shown in *figures 13.1 to 13.5* illustrates an efficient method for stepping off and getting down and stopping in balance. It is useful to have a horse that stops when you fall off, particularly if you get a foot caught in the stirrup. Hanging and dragging around usually scares hell out of a horse—and all the running and kicking gets your blood on his legs and really messes up the corral.

Fig. 13.13. The horse is locked up, sliding behind, and running in front during the third stride of the stop. It is now physically possible for the horse to keep his hind feet in the balanced-stop position. The rider's weight remains well forward as he steps to the ground.

Fig. 13.14. The horse braces with his hind feet to absorb the shock of the calf hitting the end of the rope.

Fig. 13.15. Note how the horse continues sliding behind and running in front until the forward motion halts.

It makes sense to pattern riding stops after efficient calf-roping stops. The photographs on these pages demonstrate the logic behind the use of the calf-roping stop in all types of fast-action stop work.

Sequence photographs of a top calf roper at the 1971 National Finals Rodeo show how to get it done in balance. *Figures 13.11 to 13.15* illustrate the fine art of the professional rodeo cowboy in action. With this top roper and his horse working in such unison, it is easy to understand why the Foreman method of using calf-roping horse stops on ridden horses was developed.

In the early 1960s, Casey Darnell won Senior Reining and also Calf Roping at the Colorado State Fair on his great mare Miss Fortune. Foreman observed the difference in stops in the two events. He asked Casey to assist him in a photographic analysis. Casey was willing to put both stops under the camera's eye. *Figures 13.16 and 13.17* tell the story.

By using the calf-roping stop and putting the methods to work in training, most horse-and-rider teams learn quickly. The voice command, if kept soft, will not cause a conflict in competition. The horse will learn to react to the brushing cue with the lifted reins. When he learns how to stop well, omit the touch on the neck and just raise your hand forward to the stop position. Everything else is the same.

Reaction time and rhythm cannot be emphasized enough. Wait for the reaction and then pull in rhythm with the off-lead front foot. The goal is to teach the horse to avoid the hard pulls of the bit. If a nonleverage bit is used, a sawing action can act as an enforcer, but only when the horse is nearly stopped. Mechanical hackamores and gag bits can be used as stronger tools of enforcement if the horse will not respond. 🐎

Fig. 13.16. At the Colorado State Fair in the 1960s, Casey Darnell won the AQHA reining and the RCA calf roping on Miss Fortune. Like everyone else, he learned that reining stops were different from calf-roping stops. Note the terrific strain on the mare's back when the rider sits and rares back. It would be almost impossible for her to get her hind legs up under her weight.

Fig. 13.17. Foreman saw how well Miss Fortune stopped when Casey roped calves. He asked Casey to step off her so that he could get sequence pictures of her calf-roping stop. Why couldn't riders stay astraddle and get these stops? Foreman discovered the answer through motion-picture analysis.

Fig. 13.18. Stopping is fun for the horse too. Accredited Foreman instructor Whit Parker, of Jefferson, Massachusetts, stops Summitwynds Wardance without a bridle. The rider is straight up, heels down, for security. This horse won the high-point certificate of versatility for the Greater Eastern Appaloosa Region as a three-year-old, the youngest horse ever to win it.

BALANCED STOP

Fig. 13.19. Monte Foreman stopping Barred's Ghost *(figs. 13.19–13.22).* This horse has placed high in adult and senior youth activities in Oklahoma and has qualified three times for the World Quarter Horse Show. He was a Super Horse contender for two years.

Fig. 13.20. No squeeze is used as a cue to stop the horse. Foreman does put his heels down for more leg grip and security. Note in both *fig. 13.19* and *fig. 13.20* that his hand has stayed on the horse's neck and that the horse is answering.

Fig. 13.21. Foreman raises his hands and checks the horse lightly. Ghost is running in front and sliding behind.

Fig. 13.22. Ghost is still sliding behind and running in front. The work of Barred's Ghost can be seen in several of Foreman's videotapes and training films.

14

The Rollaway from the Lead

The **rollaway from the lead** is a 180-degree turn away from the lead over the hindquarters, at a gallop, the horse coming out in the new lead going the opposite way. This is one of the three ways a horse can roll 180 degrees over the hocks and stay efficient throughout the move. It is directly related to the lead-agility needs of the horse. Over thirty years ago Foreman research discovered this move-basic and named it *rollback*. Today, for purposes of clarity, the term *rollaway* has been adopted.

In addition to the rollaway, two other move-basics to reverse the horse 180 degrees have been identified: the *same-lead roll and out the opposite lead* and the *same-lead roll*. See chapters 15 and 16 for a detailed study of each of these rolls.

Foreman photoanalysis demonstrates how a horse can be galloping in a left lead, stop quickly, and roll away from that lead, coming out in the right lead. This is a rollaway. It is the easiest method of reversing the horse 180 degrees at the gallop—easiest for both horse and rider. That is why it is taught early in training. Rolling the horse toward a fence requires less direct pull-back on the bit, and the strong turning action causes the horse to begin learning the stop response sooner. Although the balanced-stop sequence was presented ahead of roll moves in this book, in actual teaching and training, roll moves are taught first.

The rollaway is the usual way a well-balanced cutting horse reverses his direction and can be used in horse-show reining patterns.

A rollaway is always away from the lead. In training it is essential that the rider be aware of all three 180-degree-roll moves. The rollaway is the easiest roll for the horse and logically the first method taught to reverse direction at the gallop. If, however, the horse is continually rolled toward the fence, problems of anticipation ("scotching") occur. The rider with a good knowledge of move-basics can gracefully roll the horse away from the fence, change leads during the roll, and prevent many problems during arena workouts.

Fig. 14.4. The horse has rolled up with all of his weight on his leading front foot. The hind feet are airborne in this part of the stride. This is the only time a horse is able to thrust his hind feet farther up under his body, enabling him to turn over his hindquarters or stop on his hind feet. The rider's balance is forward without any weight on his seat. As you can see, if the rider's weight were back, it would prevent the horse from making his maximum stride with his hind feet.

Fig. 14.3. The rider raises his rein hands and then pulls on the horse's mouth as the off-lead front foot hits the ground. This gives the horse time to react. The rider tells the horse the direction of the turn by pulling a little harder on the right rein.

Fig. 14.5. The horse's hindquarters are well under him to balance his weight as he transfers from his left front foot to his right front foot going into a right lead. The rider has turned the horse's head slightly to the right. You can see how natural this is for the horse. The rider position is still forward, and his weight is straight up from the ground. He does *not* lean in the direction of the turn. Keeping the heels down enhances the grip from the knee down through the bottom of the rider's calf.

Fig. 14.6. Note the galloping motion of the horse's front legs as he rolls over his hindquarters going into the right lead. His head rises to help him balance, and the rider's hands move with the head motion. Coordinated rein action guides the horse to the right. The rider shifts his weight back onto his seat only after the horse's legs are well up under his body.

Fig. 14.7. The horse's front feet have completed the pivot off the ground and are preparing to come out in the right lead. The hind feet do not move or change position. The rider position is straight up from the ground, *not* leaning in the direction of the turn. The hands are still moving with the horse's head motion. The rider asks the horse to jump out by clucking, then using his left leg well back of the girth. To enforce this signal, the rider may also use the end of his reins or a bat on the horse's left hip. Always drive the hindquarters toward the desired lead (opposite side).

Fig. 14.2. Observe the difference in the position of the horse's legs. The rider's hands are still low, and the rider position is the same. All the horse's feet are airborne, and his off-lead front foot is about to strike the ground. At this point the rider says, "Whoaa." This is the preparatory stop command for the horse. It is consistent with all maneuvers requiring the horse to get his hindquarters up under him.

Fig. 14.1. *Rollaway from the lead (figs. 14.1–14.9).* Here the horse is in the left lead. Note that the left front and left hind legs lead the right front and right hind legs. The rider's hand position is low and moving in rhythm with the horse's head. The rider position is straight up with the weight carried on the stirrups. Monte Foreman on his two-year-old Thoroughbred gelding Sir Patrick.

Fig. 14.8. The horse's left front foot has gone to the ground and has rolled over to his right front foot, which is now the leading foot. In a split second both hind feet will come off the ground and the horse will move out in a right lead.

Fig. 14.9. The maneuver is completed. Note how relaxed the horse has remained throughout the movement. The right front and right hind feet are clearly in the right lead. The rider assumes a normal position, and his hands are still moving in rhythm with the horse's head.

15

The Same-Lead Roll and out the Opposite Lead ("Same-and-Out")

In the **same-lead roll and out the opposite lead** the horse rolls 180 degrees toward the lead in which he is traveling and the rider causes the horse to jump out in the opposite lead. This move was first identified while Foreman was filming the great Jimmy Williams in California. Jimmy was galloping into a spin and coming out in the other lead. It has since become an essential move-basic of the Foreman Method.

This maneuver is more difficult than a roll-away from the lead. In most training situations rolling toward the lead necessitates turning away from the arena fence. In the rollaway the fence is often a training aid. The stopping action and use of enforcement must be well thought out. Pay attention to the pivoting action of the horse. He must pivot over his hind legs, not his navel or his front legs.

The use of "same-and-outs" in training will give the rider a method to pivot away from the fence. It eliminates the problem of anticipation that occurs when doing only rollaways. This move also prepares the rider for tough competition. Having a variety of ways to roll 180 degrees assures a smoother performance, and the unexpected can be covered to look routine. The smoothness of this move-basic eliminates the need for harsh guidance and spurring. An agile and relaxed horse is the result.

Pivoting the horse one step past the original line of travel is the key to this lead selection. There are two ways to be sure of getting the correct lead: a turn toward the lead, as done here, or a collected depart. The turn technique presented here allows speed in direction change, while retaining balance. It takes more time to train a horse to perform the collected depart because it is not as natural a movement. The collected depart also slows the maneuver.

Remember the importance of the horse's head position. Without good lateral flexion the same-and-out cannot be executed smoothly or consistently. This move-basic is used to a great degree in Foreman Clinics, which specialize in teaching riders to train their own horses.

Fig. 15.4. The horse's front feet have landed on the ground, completing the first stride of his galloping movement. The rider's hands have followed with the balancing action of the horse's head. The horse prepares to lift into the second stride of the roll as the rider impulses with his lower right leg. After the horse's hindquarters have come well under him, the rider can sit down.

Fig. 15.3. The horse's hind legs are well under him with weight transferred to the hindquarters. The horse is lifting in front, rolling over his hocks. As he turns in a galloping rhythm, the rider's hands move with the horse's natural head actions. Note how the horse balances with his head and neck. The rider continues bumping with his right leg.

Fig. 15.5. As the horse rolls over his hocks, he lifts and turns his head to assist his balance. Note the effect of the coordinated rein in turning the horse's head and allowing maximum efficiency in the horse's movement. The rider position is 90 degrees to the ground—straight up—and his right leg is still on the girth, bumping the horse to make him turn.

Fig. 15.6. The horse lands with his front feet preparing to go into the air on the third stride. The rider's hand is in line with his shoulders and the horse's mouth. This procedure must be followed consistently in all stop and roll maneuvers.

Fig. 15.7. The horse is still galloping to the left over his hindquarters. He is now beginning to turn to the right, and has changed his front lead. The rider has stopped cueing with his right leg and begins to use his left leg well back, to prepare the horse to jump out in the right lead.

Fig. 15.2. The horse's hind legs are moving up under his body. Use of the coordinated rein moves the horse's head slightly in the direction of the turn. Research and experience have shown that the hand position seen here is most effective in stopping and working over the hocks. The rider's position has not changed, and there is no weight on his seat.

Fig. 15.1. *Same-lead 180-degree rollout in opposite lead (figs. 15.1–15.9).* In this sequence the horse begins on the left lead *(above)*. As in all other roll moves the rider has signaled the horse with the voice command "Whoaa" and moved his rein hand with a slight brush from the withers up the neck, throwing slack in the rein. At this point the rider suggests the direction of the turn with the reins and his right foot bumping on the girth. Pat Wyse on Chum.

Fig. 15.8. The horse's front feet come to the ground in the right lead, a quarter turn past his new line of travel. The horse's head is guided in the direction of the new lead. The rider's position remains straight up. If the rider leans into the turn, it usually causes the horse to come out disunited or in the wrong lead.

Fig. 15.9. The rider, still straight up, sits down as he pushes the horse out. To enforce the left-leg cue, a bat or long rein ends may be used on the horse's left hip to encourage him to jump out at this split second. The rider's balance is back and slightly away as he lets the horse carry him out. Note that the horse comes out in the right lead.

16

The Same-Lead Roll

The **same-lead roll,** a galloping maneuver, is a 180-degree roll in the direction of the lead. For example, the horse is in the right lead, rolls 180 degrees to the right, and comes out in the right lead. Foreman photoanalysis has demonstrated that the same-lead roll occurs continually when action demands that the rider roll his horse 180 degrees at a gallop. In shows all 180-degree rolls are sometimes called rollbacks, though in fact the horse is able to use his leads three ways: (1) the rollaway, (2) the same-lead roll and out the opposite lead, and (3) the same-lead roll.

It is important for the rider to understand the dynamics of each move-basic. The greater knowledge and ability with leads the rider has, the more versatile a performer he can be. Used in training, the same-lead roll increases the agility of both horse and rider. Stops are improved by practicing the elements of the same-lead roll. Propping in a stop is eliminated, since the horse is being turned in the direction of the lead, which forces him to flex his front legs and keep his weight on his hindquarters. It also gives the horse practice in staying in the correct lead throughout the stop sequence. Because stiff front legs and lead changing in the stop are two recurring problems that are difficult to overcome, it is necessary to include this maneuver in training. It will play an important part in bringing the horse closer to his maximum agility and versatility.

The same-lead roll is the most difficult of the 180-degree rolls, since it requires the horse to turn his head and body with minimum resistance. Accurate, coordinated lateral control must be used, and the rider position has to be exact. It is the most valuable method of making a horse retain his galloping lead movements, because he goes down into a good balanced stop. Properly learned, the roll can expand horse-handling horizons and help keep those good stops for years of smooth, trouble-free performance.

SAME-LEAD ROLL

Fig. 16.1. *The same-lead roll.* In this sequence *(figs. 16.1–16.9)* the horse is traveling in the right lead. The rider is in the normal balanced position with his weight slightly off the hindquarters. Monte Foreman on Warrior's Dream.

Fig. 16.2. The preparatory command is given in a calm voice, "Whoaa," followed by a slight raising of the rider's hand toward the horse's ears. At this point the horse should be on a slack rein. These movements may seem unnatural to the rider but are totally natural for the horse. The rider position is straight up with the heels down for more security around the barrel of the horse. The rider does not lean forward or change position as he raises his hand. Doing so causes the horse to be overbalanced on his forequarters.

Fig. 16.9. The same-lead roll is completed as the horse moves out in the right lead. The rider continues to impulse the horse with his leg. Note how the rider sits back, helping the horse come out in the correct lead.

Fig. 16.8. The horse is starting to come out in the right lead. The rider's leg position is back, to impulse the horse. If the horse is difficult to hold in lead, the rider can sit back even more than shown. It is imperative that the rider does *not* lean in the direction of the turn or too far forward, since this can cause the horse to come out in the wrong lead. Remember, the same lead in and the same lead out are the goal of this move-basic.

Fig. 16.3. Here the horse reacts to the cue. Note the stress on the pastern of the lead front foot. The hind legs are about to become airborne, which occurs only on the leading front foot. The rider guides slightly to the right with a coordinated rein but no actual pressure on the bit.

Fig. 16.4. The horse's hind feet have made a larger arc and are well up under his body. The right front leg is flexed, preparing to turn. The rider is in the raised position on the stirrups. On Balanced Ride saddles the stirrups are hung four to six inches farther forward than on ordinary saddles.

Fig. 16.5. The horse is well balanced, with his weight transferred to his hindquarters. He is in position to roll with maximum efficiency. The rider position is still raised, and he is using a coordinated rein, pulling slightly back and to the right. Note the top line of the horse. Everything is relaxed.

Fig. 16.7. The horse rolls back over his hind legs. His front legs are moving to the right with a galloping motion. The rider is straight up in the saddle; he has corrected his slight lean. The rein hand guides to the right in motion with the horse's head as the left leg bumps the horse on the girth, in rhythm with the rider's hands.

Fig. 16.6. The start of the second stride as the horse and rider come around. The right knee is flexing for the second stride. The rider can sit down after the horse's hind legs are well under him.

127

Fig. 16.11. Trophies, plaques, and ribbons won by Warrior's Dream in 1973, which included the World Championship Paint Show in Denver.

Fig. 16.10. Susan Baker on Warrior's Dream, Rocky Mountain Paint Horse Association high-point gelding, 1973, after only two shows.

17

The 360-Degree Roll

The ***360-degree roll*** involves the same move-basics as those used in other roll moves. A stopping effort must be made by the horse, thereby changing the forward motion to allow a turning action to occur. With his hind feet well under, it is possible for the horse to roll over the hocks with minimum stress and exertion.

This move in a well-trained horse can be completed in three turning strides. The entry into the move, the roll, and the depart in the same lead should flow in a continuous rhythm. The ultimate goal of this move-basic is for the horse-and-rider team to execute galloping single, double, or triple 360-degree rolls and come out in either lead, as desired, with a graceful, uninterrupted flow of movement.

The 360-degree roll is an excellent move to increase the agility of the horse and the rider's awareness of rhythmic moves. Used in a training routine, the 360-degree roll keeps the horse keen and not anticipating a specific pattern. This method of doing a 360-degree roll retains the beautiful flow of the galloping rhythm, as opposed to many reining patterns, which call for hesitating before taking the correct lead out.

The same basic principles apply in this roll move as in all others: The horse must have his hind feet balanced under him before he is turned. The rider must follow the horse's galloping rhythm with his guiding efforts, which include use of the coordinated rein, leg cues, galloping hand movement, and balanced weight. In training, use of the leg, spurs, a bat, or the rein ends acts to enforce cues when necessary. 🐎

360-DEGREE ROLL

Fig. 17.1. *The 360-degree roll (figs. 17.1–17.10).* The horse is in the right lead. His hind feet are airborne. The rider gives the preparatory command, "Whoaa." Note that when the horse is on his leading front foot both hind feet are airborne. Pat Wyse on Chum.

Fig. 17.10. The horse is coming out in the right lead, which completes the 360-degree move-basic.

Fig. 17.9. The horse is reacting by thrusting out in the right lead in answer to the command. The rider's position is straight up and back, which makes it easier for the horse to come out in the right lead. If the rider leans in, he may cause the horse to take the wrong lead.

Fig. 17.8. The horse continues to roll over the hindquarters. The rider position is still straight up—note that the horse does the leaning. At this point the rider prepares the horse to come out of the roll by clucking to him and moving his left leg back near the rear girth.

Fig. 17.2. The horse begins to react as the rider brings his rein hand toward the horse's ears in the stop position. Even with slack in the reins, the rider's hand subtly cues the horse to turn to the right.

Fig. 17.3. The horse's hind feet come off the ground as his weight is carried on the lead front foot. With the rider in the raised position the horse has maximum assistance in getting his hind feet well placed under his body. The rein hand remains in the stop position and suggests the turn to the right.

Fig. 17.4. The horse's head is turned slightly to the right, which allows him maximum agility in the turn. The balance of the rider is securely forward, with heels down and legs in the rider's groove. He uses his left lower leg on the girth to coordinate a turn to the right, while bumping in rhythm with the galloping stride.

Fig. 17.7. The horse has lifted off in front and is pivoting on the right rear leg. Note how the pivot foot supports the horse's weight. The rider's hands are in the stop position, following the galloping movements of the horse's head. Whenever the horse's hindquarters are under him, the rider can improve the horse's agility slightly by sitting down.

Fig. 17.6. The horse maintains his galloping rhythm throughout the turn. His head works with his forequarters, lowering and rising in unison. With his hands the rider follows and aids this action. If needed, enforcement can be accomplished with a spur on the girth and a bat or wide flat reins on the shoulder to motivate the turn. Remember, the leg is the signal, while the spur and bat are enforcement tools.

Fig. 17.5. The hind feet are now well set under the horse, in position for the roll. The rider's hands move with the horse's head as the horse thrusts to the right. The rider is straight up. After the hind feet are set, the rider can sit down to assist the horse in rolling over his hocks.

18

The 180-Degree Roll to the Correct Lead

The ***180-degree roll to the correct lead*** is made by rolling the horse over the hocks from a standing position and causing him to jump out in the correct lead. This move is similar to a rollaway but is made from a standing position.

The 180-degree roll to the correct lead is used in working cattle, playing polo, and riding in other competitive events in which the horse stands still and a quick reverse of direction is necessary. It is a useful training move for increasing the sensitivity of the horse and getting correct leads *(Figures 18.1 to 18.5)*.

If a horse is difficult to get into a left lead, roll him to the left and vigorously hit him on the right hip. This usually forces the horse to take the left lead.

Observe the use of the rider's hands and legs in this work over the hocks. It is the same technique used in all roll moves. Consistency of cues makes it possible for the horse to learn a variety of roll combinations easily, which increases his handiness and working ability. 🐎

Fig. 18.2. The horse begins to pivot to the left. Note the position of the rider's left hand and the straight-up position of his body. The rider may use a flat bat or long rein ends to enforce the guiding cue. A smack on the right hip is more effective than spurring to get a horse to move to the gallop. A soft voice command, such as clucking, is a training essential.

Fig. 18.3. The horse is coming out in the left lead. The rider's right leg moves back to motivate the horse to extend to the left lead. The rider's position remains straight up.

Fig. 18.4. The horse continues his galloping move to the left lead.

Fig. 18.1. ***Pick-up 180-degree roll to the left lead*** *(figs. 18.1–18.5).* Here the rider tightens the reins and tenses his legs to warn the horse to get ready to move. The roll will be to the left. The rein hand is moved to the left. The rider's right leg bumps the horse on the right girth. Monte Foreman on Barred's Ghost.

180-DEGREE ROLL TO THE LEFT LEAD

Fig. 18.5. The horse has completed the 180-degree-roll move and is galloping in the left lead. Repeat the same steps to the right for the right lead.

19
Spins

Spins are continuous 360-degree rolls over the hocks in place. The horse should be able to spin at the walk, trot, or gallop for maximum versatility. For utmost efficiency the rider should be able to spin right or left and make the horse gallop out in the lead of the spin or the opposite lead.

Competitive reining patterns call for various combinations of the spin, from multiple spins to abbreviated spins of 90 or 180 degrees. The signal to the horse and the basic balance factors are identical to those used in complete spins. As an agility-training maneuver, the spin teaches the horse to use his front legs in coordinated action while turning over the hocks.

To train a horse to spin calmly and without fear of being spurred, he can be taught a step at a time. Gradually bring the horse over the hocks at the walk by using coordinated rein action. Slightly turn the horse's head toward the direction of the spin as you pull back on the nonleverage bit. When the horse gives by making a slight pivoting action, release the reins and push the horse forward. Continue this maneuver until the horse gives willingly. This may require several brief lessons extending over a number of days.

When the horse begins to move one step freely, add additional steps, encouraging him to keep his inside hind leg in place to act as the pivot point. When the horse is going to the right, the right hind foot should remain reasonably stationary. As the horse combines the individual steps into a series of pivoting strides, begin to use more leg signal on the left girth, the bat on the left side of the neck, and less pressure on the bit. Properly trained, the horse will begin to move over the hocks on signal. This move should be taught in both directions.

Throughout training, the rider should signal the horse to prepare to spin by moving his outside leg forward. A bumping action in rhythm with the lead front foot should be used. Spinning to the right, the horse leads with his right foot as he pivots over his right rear foot. By signaling the horse as he rises to spin, the rider provides adequate reaction time for the horse to prepare for the next spinning stride. If the rider waits until the horse lands with his lead front foot, a lag in the spinning stride will occur. This lag is due to the horse's need for reaction time. To keep a rhythmic continuous spinning action, cue the horse as he lifts or is in the air with his lead front foot. The rider's weight should remain straight up or slightly back and outside.

The spin is not a natural movement for the untrained horse. Since it is an acquired move, more time must be allowed to teach it to your horse. Don't rush it. Take time to teach the horse to respond to minimum pressure.

Many potentially good reining horses are ruined by excessive spurring and knocking before the horse understands how to escape the punishment. Once a horse responds to mild aids, then speed can be added by stronger use of the bat. Remember, *the bat is the enforcer, not the cue.* 🐎

THE SPIN

Fig. 19.10. The horse has rolled over his off-lead front foot preparing to lift off with the lead front foot. The rider's hands bring the horse back and to the right, the rider using foot, leg, and bat to accelerate the spin. The bat enforces turn impulsion of the spin when used on the shoulder and neck. Always start easy with the bat and use no more force than necessary.

Fig. 19.1. *The spin* (figs. 19.1–19.10). Here the rider's position is straight up from the ground, balance slightly back, walking the horse into a right turn. The rider is guiding the horse with a coordinated rein action, which involves using the leading (direct) and bearing (indirect, or neck) reins with equal pressure. This places the horse's head in the most natural position for the spin. Monte Foreman on Sir Patrick, a three-year-old Thoroughbred.

Fig. 19.9. When the horse is well trained, his head will be turned no more than shown here for maximum efficiency. If it is turned excessively, he becomes heavy on the forehand. Canting his nose away from the turn can cause rearing, loss of rhythm, and awkwardness.

Fig. 19.8. The horse has landed on his off-lead front foot, rolling over to his lead right front foot. With his hind feet well under, it is easy for the horse to transfer his weight to his hindquarters. The rider's hands and legs maintain the rhythmic guiding to the right.

Fig. 19.2. The horse is walked tightly around to set him up for the spin, the rider using the leg on the girth and the bat on the shoulder. The rider's left leg is used to push the horse in rhythm with the hands. Actions of legs, hands, bat, or ends of reins are all synchronized with the rhythm of the horse's galloping strides.

Fig. 19.3. The horse is rolled over from his left front foot to his right front foot in preparation for lifting his forequarters, assisted by his hindquarters, which are well under him. This is the beginning of the first galloping stride of the maneuver. The rider's hand has gone to the stop position, guiding the horse slightly to the right on a snaffle bit.

Fig. 19.4. Note how the horse lifts and resets his hind feet. Foreman photo-analysis demonstrates that most horses do this when galloping in the spin.

Fig. 19.7. Continuation of the lifting, galloping rhythm is maintained as the horse raises his head to balance his body. The rider's hands gallop with the horse's head but never cease to guide the head toward the direction of the turn.

Fig. 19.6. With completion of the second stride, the rider pulls back with co-ordinated reins, which maintain pressure on both sides of the bit and bring the horse back over his hocks.

Fig. 19.5. The rhythmic use of the leg, reins, and bat to impulse the galloping stride is continued. This spin sequence was photographed during the actual training of this green colt. The rider position is straight up from the ground, **not** leaning into the turn.

Monte Foreman on Chappo Hancock.

20
Afterword

It is my firm belief that any system of teaching horse handling must be geared for the average horse and the average rider. A method of training that is built around a few exceptional horses creates an environment that will cause stress and difficulty for the average student. The system, to be adequate, must provide for rapid advancement for the above-average horse-and-rider team and a slower pace for the less athletic. Through the use of move-basics both goals can be achieved.

The need for understanding the science of move-basics becomes clear when the horse is extended to the gallop. As you have learned, the agility needs of the horse are most crucial during the galloping action. The more knowledge you have about the natural laws of motion, the easier it is to control the movements of the horse.

Each move-basic is progressive, and in these pages we have documented each one in a logical learning sequence. For example, the rider's ability to move to the raised position for the natural flying lead change prepares him to use the raised position for the stopping aspects of roll moves. The lateral movement of the horse's head in drop-to-trot lead changes follows through when he is doing any roll move. The stopping action of the roll moves prepares horse and rider for efficient stops. The methods used to perform a collected depart to the correct lead are related to collected lead changes. Each move-basic lays the foundation for more advanced maneuvers.

The overall purpose of this method of training horse and rider is to improve their athletic ability as a team. The team can then apply its newfound ability to whatever specific endeavor is desired. The move-basic technology taught in this manner will not only greatly improve the team's skills but add to the rider's enjoyment in being part of this great sport.

I hope that you have enjoyed this book. May you always ride a good horse, and may your good horse enjoy you more through your greater understanding of natural reaction horse-training science.

Adiós, amigos!

Monte Foreman

Index

Monte Foreman's Horse-Training Science,

designed by Sandy See, was set in a version of Helvetica by the University of Oklahoma Press and printed offset on 80-pound Glatfelter Offset, D-10 by Cushing-Malloy, Inc., with case binding by John H. Dekker & Sons.